WALLWORKS

WALLWORKS

CREATING UNIQUE ENVIRONMENTS WITH SURFACE DESIGN AND DECORATION

AKIKO BUSCH

FOREWORD BY MERVIN KAUFMAN, EDITORIAL DIRECTOR, *HOUSE BEAUTIFUL*

RAINCOAST BOOKS
VANCOUVER

WALLWORKS

A RUNNING HEADS BOOK

Published in Canada by
Raincoast Book Distribution Limited
112 East 3rd Avenue
Vancouver, B.C. V5T 1C8

Canadian Cataloguing in Publication Data

Busch, Akiko.
Wallworks
Includes index.
1. Walls. 2. Interior decoration.
3. Mural painting and decoration.
4. Decoration and ornament. I. Title.
NK2119.B88 1992 747′.3 C92-091159-5

ISBN 0-920417-40-X

WALLWORKS
was conceived and produced by
Running Heads Incorporated
55 West 21 Street
New York, NY 10010

Editor: Jill Herbers
Designer: Stephanie Bart-Horvath
Original Artwork: Michael Horvath
Production Associate: Belinda Hellinger

Typeset by Nassau Typographers
Color separations by Hong Kong Scanner Craft Company Ltd.
Printed and bound by C & C Offset Printing Co., Ltd.
10 9 8 7 6 5 4 3 2 1

To the memory of Mary Smart Busch

ACKNOWLEDGMENTS

My thanks first and foremost to the craftsmen, artists, designers, and architects who have contributed so greatly to this book. Their willingness to share their work despite demanding schedules and work loads is continuing testimony to their creativity and generosity of spirit.

I am grateful as well to the photographers whose work is shown here. They were unstinting in their own submissions and suggestions of projects I may never have found otherwise. Coleen O'Shea and Becky Cabaza of Bantam Books should also be thanked.

Finally, my thanks to Marta Hallett, Ellen Milionis, and Jill Herbers of Running Heads Incorporated who have been excited by this book from start to finish, and whose excitement has worked as constant, generous, and vital support and encouragement.

CONTENTS

FOREWORD

Walls have always had significance. From the time people first fashioned crude shelters for themselves, walls have been the focus of their need for warmth, visual enrichment and self-expression. The same primitive beings who documented their culture so vividly in cave paintings also hung animal skins to shut out the cold and proclaim their hunting prowess. That drive to embellish the environment has been shaped in a multiplicity of ways ever since.

It was the Chinese in the second century A.D. who created hand-painted wallpaper, a concept that took six hundred years to reach the capitals of the West. But despite its undeniable beauty and refinement, wallpaper was never intended to provide warmth. Later, descendants of the people whose homes displayed animal hides turned to tapestries, embroideries and loosely woven wool and linen fabrics, which were attached to rods and hung on hooks against stone walls, thus introducing color, pattern and the grace of notes of hospitality into Gothic life.

The Renaissance saw these textile embellishments extended. Rich brocades and damasks, no longer supported by rods, were made to cover whole walls. Other walls were hung with mirrors or covered with murals. All these techniques conspired to make walls dominant in shaping the character of a room.

The American and French revolutions marked a decrease in aristocratic patronage of the arts and, at the same time, an increased interest in decorating on the part of the rising middle classes who could not afford the extravagance of hand-painted murals or hand-carved wood paneling. Artists and craftsmen responded by producing imitative materials that achieved similar effects at much less cost. Since then, there has been a proliferation of painting techniques and wallcovering designs for use in the absence of architectural ornamentation.

Traditionally, walls meant support but also separation. If they held up ceilings and roofs, they also delineated spaces, particularly in Victorian homes. Every room was designed for a specific purpose, and the number and arrangement of rooms reflected a family's social station and conformity. Thus the floor plan of a typical Victorian house had its parlor, sitting room, dining room, breakfast room, music room, sewing room, sun room, library, bedrooms and dressing rooms. The rigidity of such a floor plan reflected the solid structure of family life at the time.

Twentieth-century technology created a kind of leveling, for it became possible for nearly everyone to enjoy, to one degree or another, the kind of decorative ornamentation that was once reserved solely for the rich. Machine printing and a new lightfastness made wallpaper not only widely accessible, but practical as well.

Respectable homes in the early twentieth century were being built on a much smaller scale, with fewer rooms and more flexibility. With the development of steel-cage construction and reinforced concrete, not all walls were required to support anything. Architects could place rooms where they were desired, walls where and if they were needed. It was not long before walls literally vanished.

In postwar America, new homes were designed around vast open spaces: living-dining rooms, dining room-kitchens, kitchen-family rooms, bed-sitting rooms, bath-fitness rooms. Then there were the so-called great rooms in which whole families cooked, dined, conversed, read, entertained and watched television. The word "togetherness" signified homes designed so that most interpersonal functions could be satisfied in one communal space. Privacy was at a premium, embellishment was barely possible, and coldness replaced coziness.

Philip Johnson's glass house, built in 1949 in New Canaan, Connecticut, is often cited as the benchmark of the Bauhaus Movement and the International Style that sought to strip architecture of ornament. "Less is more" was the dictum of Mies van der Rohe, and Johnson, an unabashed Mies disciple, created a glass pavilion that was serene, beautiful, more sculptural than architectural, and about as livable as a bell jar. His house, damned as well as praised from the moment he finished it, expressed the irreducible minimum, for it had no interior walls at all. Frank Lloyd Wright remarked that on entering it he didn't know whether to take his hat off or leave it on. Most people, he felt, would prefer to experience the difference between their indoor and outdoor worlds.

The new technology exploited by Johnson and other Bauhaus adherents resulted in strong expressions of structure but pale reflections of life. "Blatant simplification means bland architecture" was Robert Venturi's caustic demurral. "Less is a bore."

"Technological advances ultimately programmed us into a systematic way of living that was just as dictatorial as the rigidity of Victorian design," recalls Bernard M. Wharton, a young Connecticut architect. "Mies' spaces, which were so pure, have come to symbolize sterility. You don't hang fox-hunt scenes on his walls, or family portraits, or parchment paintings from your trip to Tahiti. But the truth is, people like to collect, to hang things, to personalize spaces. Is it our right as architects to dictate patterns of living or put limitations on expression?"

This question recalls the controversy that boiled up in the early '60s when CBS moved into the New York headquarters building Saarinen had designed in an almost brutalist nod to the International Style: undeniably magnificent in its time, but completely cerebral. As the employees unpacked, they were told they could not hang pictures, prints or calendars; they had to seek permission to acquire or locate plants; their desktops had to be kept free of clutter. The starkness and inhumanity of these offices on floor after floor of the skyscraper tower were in almost bizarre contrast to those of the company chairman, William Paley, who was enveloped in elegantly wood-paneled walls from which hung ornately framed samples of his art collection. The setting he inhabited could have been a century old for all the relevance it had to its austere contemporary surroundings.

"This morning my dining room was finished with green serge hanging and gilt leather, which is very handsome," wrote Samuel Pepys on an October day in 1660. Some three hundred years later, homeowners might have found this image tantalizing, for many had come to feel deprived. Bring back the leather skins and the tapestries, they cried. Give us back our walls! People longed for true privacy, separation, the option to have either when and if they wished. And they found themselves craving what could be satisfied only when they led their families over the hill to grandmother's house, which had true lived-in warmth and, invariably, walls.

But if there is a growing repudiation of the International Style, does that mean that dwellings and commercial buildings will once again become warrens of dark, confining spaces as a reaction against the use of ornament? Certainly not, says Barnard Wharton: "People are looking to what seemed to work a hundred years ago, but this doesn't mean today's architects are simply regurgitating nineteenth-century ideas. Since walls in many instances need not be structural, enormous variations are possible: glass walls, rice-paper walls, half walls, walls that don't quite reach the ceiling, architectural elements that suggest the presence of walls."

Wharton cites a 1,500-square-foot house in Basking Ridge, New Jersey, that he and his partner, Allan P. Shope, designed in 1986: "It was our purpose to create a sense of privacy without interrupting the flow of modest space, and not every element that serves as a wall actually is one. Starting at the front of the house, you move through a lattice arch, which screens the entrance. Inside you pass the stairwell, which acts as a wall to partly enclose the foyer. Beyond it a double fireplace creates a division between the living and dining rooms, and a waist-high counter separates the kitchen from the dining area. At the rear of the house a glass wall acts as a light tower, linking upper and lower levels and—more important—admitting sunlight and the flavor of the outdoors without forfeiting privacy. Walls are central to the architecture, even if you don't perceive them strictly as walls."

Another young architect and clearly no Mies disciple, Walter Chatham of New York City sees an extension of what he calls the Bauhaus' "ultimate minimalism" in today's sheetrocked wall, but with an opposite reaction. "It is completely consistent," he says. "If you roller-paint it, you have a flat, dull surface that either disappears or cries out for embellishment. And most people have discovered that minimalism is expensive: The workmanship must be flawless."

Flawless workmanship is more than costly nowadays; it is virtually unattainable. Also, people tend to shy away from perfection, responding more positively to flaws, intentional or otherwise. The imperfect stucco wall carries with it implied warmth, for example, because it suggests hands-on work. This may explain why there is such interest in the various "distressing" and fool-the-eye techniques that are discussed in this book. All disguise acknowledged flaws and imperfections, and also add texture, dimension and variation to bland surfaces.

"Who built these walls made known
 The music of the mind . . . "

Gerard Manley Hopkins' lines aptly describe the ideas and aspirations of a new generation of laymen and professionals who do not regard walls as outmoded impediments to creative initiative and free-flowing space, but as the means not only to define space but also to control it. Walls are intrinsic to today's design needs and the never-ending thrust for personal expression—just as they were when cavemen painted those colorful impressions of a puzzling external world.

MERVYN KAUFMAN

INTRODUCTION

Our age is, without a doubt, a visual one. The contemporary taste for vitality in color, texture, pattern, and lively graphics is in part a strong response to modernist austerity, which for decades has banished ornamentation as superfluous, pointless, even criminal. But, the revived appeal for ornament is also ongoing evidence of the human taste for decoration. Ornament has always had a hold on the popular imagination. It is a hold that has become stronger in contemporary culture.

Because of this emphasis on decoration, we have become visually literate. We are surrounded by new images, and we often learn and communicate visually. Television, tabloid headlines, advertising graphics, and extravagant special effects in film all beg our attention. The more aggressive their terms, the more successful they are. So we are visually aware, if not visually sophisticated. It is appropriate that the design world should take note and direction from this graphic intensity because it is the designers and architects who bring to this surfeit an order, refinement, and sensibility.

With the acceptance of ornamentation and decoration in architecture has come a new vitality in home design. Walls are not simply the means by which space is structured, but instead have become blank canvases for embellishment as well. New directions in design refute the modernist proposal that the space, surface, and structure of architecture are best served by asserting function cleanly, purely, and without adornment.

Along with the renewed interest in home decoration comes a revival in the practice of age-old decorative traditions. Architectural ceramics, stenciling, trompe l'oeil, faux surfaces, wallpaper, tapestries, and wallhangings are all appearing with new vigor. While these decorative traditions may have been dismissed by modernists as being extraneous and lacking in aesthetic integrity, each has a long history in the decorative arts which speaks for its enduring human appeal.

Yet if such traditions have a history to them, how they are practiced often does not. While many artisans pride themselves on drawing on the heritage of their art in design, pattern, material, tools, and application, as many others choose to deviate. Contemporary graphics and images, as well as new technologies, all bring new life to old traditions. Random geometric patterns, expressionist spontaneity, and photo-realist landscapes are all reflected on the surfaces created by contemporary designers. Artists, craftsmen, designers, and architects alike are attuned to a new set of references. These are the graphics of popular culture at large. Design no longer exists in a calculated and theoretical realm; instead, popular culture provides motifs, images, colors, and textures which can be assimilated into contemporary design. Ceramist Dorothy Hafner, for example, notices hot pink bubblegum embedded in tar and repeats the colors and images in her architectural ceramics and housewares; computer graphics suggest pattern sequences for tilework and textiles; typography, even graffiti, become design elements as well as graphic tools.

As one might suspect from all this, there is a good deal of give-and-take. Decorative arts happily beg, borrow, and steal from one another. They merge and mesh without limit. Pompeian murals provide inspiration to some of the same artists that are influenced by Jackson Pollock's field paintings. Classicism has graceful collisions with abstract expressionism. Anything goes, so long as it is applied with wit, refinement, innovation, and artistry.

Airbrushes, spray paints, sandblasted glass, dayglow colors, metallic paints, and Mylar papers are only some of the new materials that are available to contemporary craftsmen. Materials and processes developed for industry filter down to artisans and designers whose subsequent applications may be more creative than anything in the minds of those who developed the product. Corian, for example, was a material developed by Du Pont in the early 1970s. A solid and nonporous synthetic surfacing material, it has the appearance of stone or marble, yet it may be worked like wood. It can be carved and shaped into a unique paneled surface.

It is with the innovative use of materials and processes made available through modern technology that some of the most compelling surfaces are achieved. Age-old traditions such as trompe l'oeil murals or stenciling on a border achieve a more contemporary sensibility when new applications and newly developed materials are used.

Moreover, there are few rules in application. Part of the beauty of contemporary design lies in its capacity to bring together seemingly disparate elements. Patterns, textures, and colors no longer need to match in the tidy arrangements they once did. Replacing them is a more creative, inventive way of combining color, texture, and pattern for one-of-a-kind designs.

Walls uncovered by archaeologists in the chambers of ancient Persian mosques were inlaid with many thousands of shards of glass mirror, fragments that reflected the passing world. Likewise, contemporary design and decoration is a mirror of our own world, and our perceptions of it. Such reflections are shown in this book. They are energetic, exhuberant, and vital. Though the walls certainly support ceilings or divide space, they also represent blank canvases to designers, artisans, and architects. The walls of residential spaces shown here point out how innovation can and does begin at home.

There are as many approaches to designing homes as there are individuals who live in them; as many designs as there are needs, desires, and whims. What all of them point to is an approach to design that takes into account man's enduring attraction to the decorated surface.

CHAPTER
1
COLOR AND PATTERN

For this L-shaped New York apartment, architect Steven Holl devised an interior horizon line—a 5/8-inch brass channel—to connect the open areas of the space. The strong horizontal lines directly juxtapose the stronger verticals of the urban skyline outside. Both the pattern of the line and the colors used to place it work to give the room an impressive presence.

Color structures the New York loft of architect Alan Buchsbaum. The layering of pastels is punctuated by the stocky red legs of the granite-topped tables, making for a medley of color and surface. The shimmering surface of the pressed tin ceiling reflects the play with color and infuses the room with even more hues.

The reappearance of color in surface design is a refreshing and welcome event. Color is a language spoken internationally. Though it does elicit personal responses and therefore its translations may be highly individual, it also conveys precise messages much as any language. For example, because the retina discerns yellow more rapidly than it does other hues, yellow is often used to signal caution or danger; because warm reds complement skin tones, they are considered friendly colors, augmenting self-confidence and communication. Some colors evoke warmth and passion; others, coolness and passivity. There *are* universals; we *do* have cultural and historical associations with color.

Still, the colors of the spectrum remain a matter of individual preference. Despite their acknowledged psychological associations, how they affect us is a subtle matter that has much to do with individual judgment. A deep blue that might be soothing to one person may appear excessively somber or gloomy to another. So it is only by acknowledging that our responses to color are a matter both of science and of the more mercurial qualities of human perception and behavior, that we can begin to understand its effects on us. Designers and architects are finding ways to measure and balance these inexact quantities for provocative and engaging surface effects.

What they have discovered is that the application of color need not necessarily be purely ornamental. Color can be used to structure space as well. Classical applications of color in domestic architecture placed darker hues on the floor, then gradations of lighter hues on the walls, and finally, the palest

Chillida

An elevator–entry foyer, left, has been elaborately painted and patterned by artist Nancy A. Kintisch in freehand geometrics. While Kintisch's patterns and designs have no direct translations, their neat rows and repetitions of symbols make for private, and playful, hieroglyphics.

Tim Street-Porter and Annie Kelly have painted the upper portions of their walls a deep blue underscored by a strip of red, below. The bands of color work to define the shape of the room. They also emphasize other horizontal lines found in the room, such as those of table surfaces, mullion windows, and picture frames. The strong horizontals that are thus established make for a serene and solid interior setting.

shades on the ceiling. Such applications tended to reflect the gradations of color found in the natural landscape. Designers and architects also observed that dark colors convey weight, while paler colors evoke a material lightness. To follow this color equation in architecture and design reinforces the natural tendencies of human perception.

The new emergence of color as a design tool does not necessarily conflict with the principles of modern design. Although contemporary architects and designers may deviate from the more rigid formulas of their classicist predecessors, they pay no less attention to the visual structure color may pose. While engaging the senses, color can be used to define planes and their relationships to each other. Color can be applied to connect space, or to separate it. Color can define as clearly as it decorates; it can order space as well as embellish it. Color, reconsidered, has a structural value.

Painter Lesley Achitoff has used a palette of the palest pastels to create a mottled effect on a kitchen wall, right. Applying the paint with a roller dipped continually in different shades of off-white, she has created a gentle surface texture and even gentler play with color that comes quietly to life. Although the eye must search for the faint and irregular patterning she has created, it is amply rewarded.

Lesley Achitoff has contrasted her pastel stipled effect in a checkerboard with bold black and white lettering, above. Press type is applied in random patterns to spell not words, but strong patterning instead. It is not a new idea that typography can be used purely for graphics rather than as a tool of communication, but its application here is surely inventive.

Craftsmen of Evergreene Painting Studios worked to recapture their client's childhood fantasy, right. The client had recalled from his childhood the metallic gold paper used to wrap candy, and asked the studio to re-create the effect on his dining room walls. Evergreene complied by using a variety of gold leafs—fourteen, eighteen, and twenty-two carat golds were applied in shades of lemons, pale golds and white golds, red and pink golds. The varied hues appeared to add age to the gold surface, antiquing it while making it a somewhat opulent recollection of youth.

Photographer Tim Street-Porter and painter Annie Kelly have used a horizontal band in varying colors with a regular stripe waving through it in place of the decorative molding, known as a "chair rail," found in more conventional and traditional interiors, above. Chair rails were decorative bands installed to prevent chairs from tipping onto plaster walls and marring their surfaces. Here, the decorative band uses color, rather than molding, as ornament and accent, and in so doing updates established decorative tradition so often in need of change.

While cinderblock architecture is ordinarily relegated to the garage, in this case it makes for an elegant interior, right. The firm of Dimitri Bulazel AIA Architects used standard concrete block, but had a warm-brown pigment added to the concrete aggregate as it was being mixed at the plant. Its rosy hues make for a warmer interior surface, and they are brought out all the more by surface-mounted heating and ventilating ducts painted with a bright pink enamel.

Horizontal bands of vivid blue signal the entry to a private residence on Lake Charles, Louisiana, opposite page. Designed by Lonnecker and Papademetriou Architects, the bands of color evoke the high-water marks and shifting tide lines of the exterior landscape; these nautical colors are found in coastal regions throughout the country and the world. The architects found that a greater depth and resonance of color could be achieved by mixing pigment directly in the stucco, rather than painting the stucco afterward. They subsequently selected three tones of blue and repeated them in different mixtures for the different bands.

Color may also influence the perceived size of objects. Often, brighter and more intensely colored objects will appear to be larger than they actually are, while darker colors may work seemingly to diminish size. In interior design, color can be used to set apart a plane, to bring in a wall, or to lower a ceiling.

In considering color application, there are three basics—hue, meaning the position of the color on the spectrum or color wheel; value, meaning its lightness or darkness; and intensity, meaning its brightness. A sensitivity to these distinctions is intrinsic to the understanding of color and to the evaluation of its effect on the environment, and of course, on other colors.

The fact that the liberal use of color has returned to interior surfaces does not mean that it is necessarily bright colors that are being used. While the brilliant supergraphics in favor during the 1960s did promote bright, primary shades, these have since been subdued by the pale pastels of postmodernism, the iridescent metallics made available through earlier industrial uses, or by subtle accents of color on pale surfaces.

There is a variety of colors and applications used, since this revival is not in any way a narrow trend. While fashion design may observe seasonal trends in color, architecture and interior design have a permanence and cost in our lives that discourages it. The decisions we make about decorating the places in which we live must have an enduring value. Says James Stockton in his *Designers Guide To Color 2*, "The most successful color combinations are usually personal and original, muted and subdued. A sense of scale and emphasis applies to color just as it does to size proportion and position in art and music. That is, a small patch of bright color placed next to pale or grayed colors can accentuate their contribution."

Enormous, natural ocean sponges dipped in black paint were used by painter Pamela Margonelli to produce a dramatic, mottled effect, left, one she humorously refers to as "the poodle print." The black sponging was applied over an undercoat of different bright hues.

Pamela Margonelli applied varying shades of blue tints over a metallic silver undercoat to achieve a surface of luminescence and depth, above. She then steelwooled the surface, and scratched it with metal implements for the random drawings and designs which compose its surface.

While a coat of flat, mossy green paint was applied over an undercoat of gold paint, it nevertheless allows the layer of gold to shimmer through, left. Pamela Margonelli then graffitied through the top layer a series of leaves, cubes, and other random images for the enigmatic hieroglyphics. The result is not writing on the wall so much as it is evocative scribbling.

The austerity of an armchair by Le Corbusier is juxtaposed by the more lyrical rainbow hues of a wall painted by Pamela Margonelli. Margonelli applied washes of watercolors in various tints and hues, using more shades of yellow near the windows to evoke illusions of sunlight. The different shades bled into each other; the wall was then beaten with rags and scribbled and scratched by hand (and fingernails) for an uneven and irregular surface effect. All in all, however, the interior is one of serenity and calm.

Along with the application of color in contemporary design has come the use of pattern. In challenging the austerity of modernism, the contemporary decorative arts have recognized and are celebrating again our natural attraction to pattern. And pattern has a capacity equal to color to elicit strong emotional responses. Whether it is the interwoven repetition of branches on a tapestry border, a series of geometric incisions on wall tiles, or the stylized florals of wallpaper or fabric, pattern enchants us. Whether a pattern is formed by images that identify, narrate a story, or act in a purely decorative capacity, it can be a captivating and dazzling reminder that repetition is implicit in our lives from the moment we begin to breathe.

Perhaps in response to the severity of machine-age aesthetics, we are as captivated by the broken pattern as we are by strict pattern itself; we are as intrigued with the irregularity of pattern as with its regularity. The use of pattern is now less structured and more lyrical. Patterns are established to be subtly broken; geometrics run softly askew; precise grids are drawn only to dissolve. In their rediscovery of pattern, artists and designers are applying not a precise and calculated mathematics, but a more human touch of the random, the unexpected, the spontaneous. Pattern accommodates irregularity.

Color and pattern together have reemerged with a new vitality in the space and on the surface of contemporary design. There are few rules, no prescribed palettes. If there is writing on the wall, its inscriptions are in a variety of languages and translations. Design dogma has been replaced by a sense of invention and a sense of humor. With both their private evocations and the more universal responses they elicit, color and pattern are perhaps the most powerful design tools we have. The designs shown in this book are graceful and provocative evidence of this fact.

CHAPTER
2
TROMPE L'OEIL AND FAUX FINISHES

The unique illusion created by trompe l'oeil and faux surfaces is shown in this hallway leading to a Romanesque foyer. Tromploy, Inc. installed a deceptive limestone wall, along with rich malachite trim and marble moldings which are also painted, rather than the real thing. Visitors often try to brush aside the vessels that appear to have been tossed to the floor, which has been painted in brilliant red and blue swirls to give the impression of a fantasy marble.

Master of trompe l'oeil and illusionistic painting Richard Haas has recreated the mottled marbles, the porticos, courtyards, vistas, and the ornate decorative detailing of an Italian villa in this New York City loft. Exposed pipes participate in the fantasy, underscoring the humor implicit in many trompe l'oeil murals.

Throughout history, deception has proved to be a subject of nearly unlimited human appeal. Fooling one another is an undeniable human trait. Fortunately, there are such outlets as the decorative arts that permit one to practice this folly without the malice usually associated with it. When practiced with wit and artistry, a lie can bring equal pleasure to both the deceived and the deceiver. This, at least, is the case with painted finishes.

Faux marbre Greek pottery dates to 2200 B.C. The glories of the holy Roman Empire, it seems, rested on multicolored *faux marbre* plaster columns as picturesquely, if not as solidly, as they might on more substantial pillars of the real thing. The reasons behind the appeal of the deceptive surface in antiquity were much the same as they are today. Often it was the high cost and impracticality of carting expensive materials across continents simply to decorate one's home that prompted the commission of the painted surface. Occasionally its use answered more pragmatic concerns—the foundation and structure of St. Peter's in Rome, for example, were unable to support walls of solid marble, so the real marble was said to extend only for about twenty feet, while the remainder was simply painted to match. Likewise at Versailles, *faux marbre* was used alongside the real thing in those areas where the full weight of stone could not be supported.

The pastoral Tuscan landscape in this bathroom, left, was actually hand-painted by Thomas Masaryk with oils and glazes. The brilliant sky was achieved by applying gold leaf over a vermillion base, then scratching the surface, and finally applying several coats of glaze. Masaryk also used sea sponges, rags, and rubber slices to simulate surfaces of rose marble and porfido verde for the lower panels of the walls.

Gary Finkel and Clyde Wachsberger of Tromploy, Inc. have installed a patch of painted sky and a column fragment in this bathroom, right. Both the pale colors, and the illusion itself, work to open up the space.

Both the flowers and the marble niche they rest in have been hand-painted by artist Lillian Kennedy. The still life is painted on a piece of canvas, which can subsequently be glued to the wall.

But the reasons for faking it are not always simply to replicate the real thing. Often the fake explores possibilities in form and color that are more limited in the real material. The contemporary decorative arts award greater recognition to such flights of fancy. The range and variety of these picturesque deceptions, then, is great, and they can be divided into three categories: The first is trompe l'oeil, the illusion that tricks the eye with its imagined perspectives and true-to-life forms and shadows; the second is the faux finish—painted surfaces that appear to duplicate the colors and textures of marbles, woods, stones, and other real materials; and the third is the faux finish that takes greater liberties, suggesting textures and finishes of materials imagined rather than real.

The origins of illusionistic trompe l'oeil painting lies with the ancient Greeks, possibly in conjunction with the development of stage sets for their theater. But as such scene painting moved from the stage to a wider audience, its decorative appeal was recognized to be as great as its deceptive appeal; forced perspectives made rooms seem larger than they might be. They created windows with vistas and views of fragrant gardens where there might only be a dark courtyard; they brought brilant blue skies with the feeling of light and air to rooms with low, confining ceilings; and they made rare marbles and malachites of wall panels and ceilings. Entire atmospheres, periods, and places could be wielded by a paintbrush. Painted objects assumed a solid, three-dimensional weight and form. Although the subjects of most trompe l'oeil paintings are lyrical, pastoral scenes, the fact is that creating them was, and still is, nearly a science. Imprecise shading, inconsistent light sources, and distorted perspectives will undermine the effect of trompe l'oeil, and its success is dependent on the mastery of the complicated techniques involved.

Faux finishes are in an entirely separate category. Rather than illustrating entire scenes and landscapes, the faux finish simply duplicates, with paints and glazes, the surface of marble, stone, wood, tortoiseshell, malachite, lapis lazuli, or any number of other very real materials. Brushes and airbrushes, sponges, squeegees, rubber stamps, combs, and even a notched windshield wiper are only some of the tools that can be used

The door used by a New York City jewelry designer in her home was located in a Greenwich Village antique shop, and while the trompe l'oeil has not been dated, it is, she says, "at least fifty years old." The quiet folk art imagery of the still life on the illusionistic shelves is juxtaposed by the whimsical entrance of the cat from the cupboard door below.

The illusion of a weatherbeaten limestone wall in a dining room has been created by Serpentine studio with oil paint on a plaster surface, above. The stormy sky hovering overhead is actually airbrushed acrylic.

Artist Michael Thornton-Smith has recreated the interior of a New Jersey home in faux marbre*, right. While the floor is constructed of quite real granite, the marbles of the columns, column bases, moldings, and the curved sheetrock wall are all painted illusions. Slightly altered from reality, these marble effects are highly imaginative. In turn, the hues of the marble column bases match that of the granite floor.*

to visually recreate the veins of marbles, the burls and grains of wood, the mottled lustre of lapis lazuli, or the precise inlays of ivory. These finishes are often found on single pieces of furniture, but they are as applicable to entire walls. For expansive areas, the finish is often painted on canvas, which is then applied, as wallpaper might be, to the wall.

And finally, there is the more imaginary surface finish. While they may have occasional, faint references to the real, material world, they are in fact, miniature landscapes of the fantastic. There is, for example, the wall of quarry rock painted by the craftsmen of Tromploy, Inc. It is resplendent with veins of turquoise, gold, and silver, and is clearly oblivious to the fact that such precious gems are not to be found in veins of quarry rock. "We *like* to do things that don't exist in nature," the craftsmen explain, and their work illustrates the beauty possible in such perversity. The painted finishes include slabs of *faux marbre* whose colorations reflect the colors used elsewhere in the interior more than they do any found in the natural world; or the irregular patterns and swirls that might resemble malachite except for the cobalt blue tones that have replaced the brilliant green of the stone; or a bamboo finish rendered in metallic glaze. Such painted finishes are superficiality at its finest. All of these are exquisite imposters that demonstrate that with the proper amount of wit and skill, anything goes in this creative category of the painted finish.

Contemporary mural painters often will use more than one of these techniques in a single mural. A pastoral landscape may be framed by an illusion of molding in a fantasy marble. Or a regular faux granite wall may have just a few panels or stripes of tortoiseshell in an incongruous green or blue. Incongruity abounds, and this, perhaps, is what most distinguishes the contemporary painted finish. These are bizarre combinations that play not only with our perceptions of what is real and what is unreal, but point out as well that what lies in the world of fact can happily and picturesquely coexist with what lies in the world of fantasy.

The question of value remains, however. Which has more of it? A marble wall or a plaster wall painted by craftsmen to resemble it? The question can only really be answered by the vagueries of personal aesthetic preference. Yet that it is raised at all is testimony to the fine art and craft of the painted finish. The late Isabel O'Neil, a master of the craft, said "Painted finishes owe their existence to the fact that men always want things more precious than they can afford." But it is also only human to want to put one over. And putting one over with gesso and gilt is surely an artful and altogether blameless way to do so.

The romantic landscapes of the murals for a dining room in Charleston, S.C., left, have been painted by Richard Gillette and Stephen Shadley and are based on nineteenth-century French wallpaper. "It was just too obvious to apply the paper," explains Gillette. "Besides, I'm a painter." The naturalistic views also bear some relation to the real landscape: The house actually does have views of a river and the crumbling marble ruins of the murals have their counterpart in the remnant architecture of the Deep South.

Mural painter Virginia Crawford has recreated a moment of Versailles for a New York client who aspired to share Louis XIV's view of the sculpture garden, right. The marble patterns were taken from Versailles, as were the dramatic Venetian reds, the deep blues, and emerald greens. If anything, Crawford admits, some colors were toned down and made less dramatic, so as to lead the eye down the vista of the statue garden.

The soft illusions painted by Richard Gillette, right, are based on a quite private interpretation of Pompeian murals; indeed, they are loose renditions of Venetian architecture rather than direct translations. Gillette's references are ancient and eclectic—a fading mural works with an eighteenth-century German sofa and an Italian stone garden table. There is an overlay of different periods of art and culture. Gillette layers illusions, one upon the other; history, meaning 79 A.D., does not so much repeat itself here as it overlaps.

The standard white porcelain tiles in Richard Gillette's kitchen have been painted as more exotic marbles, opposite page. That the marble has crumbled in some places is in keeping with the Pompeian spirit of the entire loft. And that the crumbling appears to have exposed an earlier frescoe is again part of Gillette's historical layering.

CHAPTER
3
STENCILED SURFACES

The historical associations of stenciling are evident in designer Leslie Ann Powers's use of an eighteenth-century pattern to ornament the dining room of a house in Connecticut from the same period. The tassel and bell motif, by American Colonial artist Moses Eaton, has a shading, subtlety, and dimension that is unusual for most Colonial patterns.

Laura Torbet painted the muted hills and sky of a dining room mural in freehand. The dancers frolicking across, however, repeat themselves by stencil. Their varying positions and colors obscure the fact that a limited number of forms has been used repeatedly. Torbet's combination of stenciled and freehand images demonstrate a contemporary approach to an ancient tradition.

For the last thirteen centuries, and probably a good deal longer, craftsmen have used cutout patterns to apply designs onto cloth, wood, metal, and other materials. There is evidence that craftsmen of primitive cultures cut holes in leaves through which they applied pigment to repeat simple patterns. The process was refined somewhat with the invention of paper around the first century A.D., and subsequently the Chinese found that stenciling was an efficient way to decorate silk as well. The Japanese enhanced the process by including in their patterns stylized motifs drawn from the natural world.

In Europe, stenciling was used for wallpapers, book illustrations, and to ornament furniture and textiles. By the mid-eighteenth century, the art of stenciling flourished in Colonial America with crude geometric patterns giving way to imitations of elaborate French wallpapers. Floors, walls, borders, and ceilings were ornamented with flora and fauna of all sorts, not to mention the patriotic imagery that abounded—stars, flags, and stylized American Eagles. Designs in this period of Colonial folk art were executed in simple shapes and stark colors—deep reds, greens, dark blues, and blacks on pale backgrounds such as buff, yellow, pale pink, or blue. For the most part, the work was done by journeymen who, for a small fee and board, might stencil a grapevine across a ceiling or scatter maple leaves across the floor. Floorcloths, windowshades, bedhangings, and tablecloths all were stenciled as were all manners of tinware, tables, beds, benches, and even pianos.

The allures of stenciling are manifold, but most obvious are its efficiency and economy—in both cost and labor—of reproduction. For large expanses, it is the means by which a single motif can be easily repeated. The cutouts permit the reproduction and standardization of often delicate designs that might otherwise be possible only through more laborious freehand painting. Stencils also permit delicate designs, by master artisans, to be reproduced by less-experienced apprentices.

Artist Lynn Goodpasture stenciled this vine-pattern design, right, in 1980. Although it is an original, it evokes the feeling of an eighteenth-century design. Used around the fireplace in one size, and along the top border of the wall in another, it demonstrates the way a single pattern may be altered and adapted to ornament different areas.

Chicago architects Thomas H. Beeby and Kirsten Peltzer Beeby used ornate stenciling in primary colors to decorate the wood-paneled walls of a one-room schoolhouse converted to a country retreat in Monroe, Wisconsin, left. Their motifs are stylized lilies and carnations, roses, sunflowers, and birds—all natural images drawn from the patterned art of Pennsylvania Dutch, as well as from the handwork of the local Swiss and German craftspeople. The sky blue trim and green wainscotting work to further reinforce the stylization of the natural landscape.

But the appeal of stenciling is not simply the ease with which it may be applied to an expansive wall. Stenciling is equally suited to small border areas and moldings, and often, its lesser application brings sufficient accent decoration to an interior. A little can actually go a very long way. The charm of stenciling is in its sense of economy.

Stenciling has a more subtle fascination as well. The impulse to decorate in an ordered series or pattern has an organic source. Its evocation of rhythm and its observance of the laws of proportion express a human impulse—the need for order and logic. The beat of the heart, the cycles of the seasons, the ebb and flow of tides—all of these demonstrate pattern in the natural world. It is not surprising that the recognition of order in the natural world should find expression in design.

The contemporary reemergence of stenciling recognizes both this universal appeal and its rich cultural tradition in American folk art. Still, its practice in contemporary design has its own deviations. Traditional stenciling tended to express a sense of regularity; precise geometric motifs repeated themselves in exact patterns. Contemporary stencilers, however, are more apt to dispel this regularity. Motifs may repeat themselves, but often in random and improvisational arrangements. Rigid geometric patterns may be established only to be disrupted by an evocative expressionist design.

The motifs themselves have changed as well. While the bells, birds, flowers, stars, and pineapples so popular in traditional stenciling remain the subject matter of some contemporary craftsmen, others use more personal and idiosyncratic imagery. The teacups and measuring spoons of Laura Torbet's work are one example of this play with motif.

The use of color has also shifted. Whereas traditional stenciling used rich, bright colors, many modern craftsmen use a more subtle palette. Gradations of softer colors have a delicacy that we do not associate with traditional work. In addition, shapes are often stenciled with less distinct outlines; subtle colors and edges may suggest shapes, but often it is in a less emphatic manner than earlier stenciled images. Often, contemporary stenciled surfaces combine some of these newer

Vividly colored teacups and measuring spoons are scattered across the surface of stenciler Laura Torbet's kitchen cabinets, left, not only decorating their surface but suggesting their contents as well. The playful images and irregular patterns of Torbet's designs demonstrate an altogether refreshing and less structured approach to the art of stenciling than traditional methods have dictated.

The elaborate red and green paisley pattern, adapted from antique Indian patterns, was created by stenciler Cile Lord and designer Gina Beadle for a renovated barn, above. Above it is a softer trellis and vine design.

Architect Robert Venturi has always extolled the glories of the decorated surface, and nowhere is this more apparent than in the home he shares with architect Denise Scott Brown. Dining and living rooms have all been stenciled with patterns created by Venturi—scattered constellations of stars of different sizes, a floral pattern with varying repeats, and subtle geometrics for the dining area. Along with the patterning of rugs underfoot, the collection of prints on the wall, and the various slipcovers and upholstery, the inventive stencil patterns make for a graphic extravaganza, a rich compendium of surface design.

MICHAEL ANGELO · SOANE ·

elements: a single wall might be ornamented with both freehand painting and stenciling, the latter of which has been executed with a less regimented order and in more subtle colors.

The contemporary art and craft of stenciling continues a long and rich tradition. As in the evolution of any design history, it reflects not only its own traditions but also the aesthetics of the culture from which it currently emerges. Some contemporary artists and craftsmen delight in practicing the art with its traditional structure and repetition; others choose to distort the measured repetitions of traditional stenciling in more random arrangements of pattern and motif; and others still, adhere to its structure and frequency and introduce subtle variations, instead, through a play with color. Gently or more vigorously, the ancient traditions in the art of stenciling are pushed, pulled, attended to, and deviated from. Most of all, they continue their decorative flights of fancy.

In a kitchen designed by Hariet Eckstein, one is confronted with an ornate landscape of Chinoiserie. The pagodas, bridges, trees, rocks, and flowers are all based on images created by the French eighteenth-century master of Chinoiserie, Jean Pillement; they are images which stencil artist Cile Lord located in archives of the Cooper Union Library in New York. The diaper pattern—the small geometric designs—surrounding these are adapted from eighteenth-century French fabric design. Eckstein and Lord combined six of these patterns and Lord executed these in colors that correspond to the Chinoiserie images. The panels can be folded back.

CHAPTER 4

TILED SURFACES

The cool convenience of tile lends itself beautifully to kitchen walls such as this one. Architect Dan Phipps has used tiles that have been spattered and handpainted by Dish Is It, a firm that specializes in custom work. The irregular splashes of neutral earth tones of the "Sahara" pattern were created to resemble the surface of the granite countertop they accompany.

Architectural tiles are among the oldest building materials known to man. Archeological sites of the Persian, Byzantine, Arab, and Turkish Empires testify to their lasting beauty, as do the splendors of Renaissance architecture. Throughout the history of design, tiles have been used to ornament walls, doorways and gates, pave courtyards, and to roof villas. From top to bottom, tiles have been used through the ages as surface structure and ornament.

The size, shape, color, and endless patterns of architectural tiles make for both decorative and durable surface design. But despite their structural practicality, their durability, and the ease with which they may be cleaned and maintained, it is their use as ornament that is most remarkable—from the decorative panels of the Orient in which the complex, geometric interlocking of hexagonal and star-shaped tiles evoke both a mathematical and mystical sensibility, to the less abstract and more pictorial ornament of blue and white Dutch tiles. Rather than being a geometric composition in which complex patterns are devised, repeated, interrupted, and broken, these murals constructed from tiles are less mathematical and more lyrical, or illustrative.

Ceramic tiles are a mixture of clay and water that has been shaped into slabs and fired at high temperatures. They can be glazed from matte to satin to high gloss finishes, and decorated or left untreated. Vitreous tiles, natural and unglazed, are used often for applications on the floor simply because they are not slippery. Nonvitreous tiles, glazed with a transparent or opaque coating, are more

Ceramic artist Dorothy Hafner has handpainted commercial, white earthenware tiles for a wall installation titled "Key West," far left. The bright colors and sharp geometrics of her designs would seem to invite pattern; yet they happily abandon it for a more exuberant arrangement. Some tiles seem to connect with those they are adjacent to, others stand alone, and others remain blank for momentary visual relief. All in all, they make for a lively and innovative tile treatment.

Ordinary commercial tiles of a kitchen backsplash have been enlivened by Dorothy Hafner's handpainted tiles, left. This installation demonstrates how as few as four handpainted tiles can bring color and originality to a kitchen surface.

Painter and ceramic artist Joyce Kozloff draws upon a rich reservoir of cross-cultural references in her hand-painted tile work, opposite. Pattern and design found in Turkoman carpets, Celtic manuscripts, Chinese porcelain, and French lace all appear in her diverse, brilliantly painted tiled surfaces. The precise interlocking of stars and hexagonal tiles framing this fireplace has a mathematical Eastern influence that is juxtaposed by a less restricted color palette.

Standard commercial wall tiles have been used here by OKG Architects to create a restrained but elegant design for a fireplace wall, right. The stripe of deep blue visually connects the area to the pale blue walls around the fireplace, while the grid of black and white tiles elegantly sets it apart. The cool color palette and subdued geometry is juxtaposed by the flicker and heat of the flames.

decorative. Their color, however, has been fired in a thin glaze rather than being baked through, and such tiles are used primarily for wall treatments, as heavy traffic or cold temperatures may crack them. White body earthenware tiles, which take colors vividly and accurately, and can be coated with transparent glazes, absorb decoration the most easily, and hence are the most frequently used for wall applications.

The contemporary rekindling of interest in architectural tiles looks to handmade, hand-decorated tiles as well as to machine-made commercial tiles; or in some instances, to commercial tiles that have been decorated by hand. How craftsmen and artists shape and decorate tiles and how these are then used by architects and designers is ample evidence that an ancient decorative tradition is enjoying new interest.

Handmade and handpainted tiles obviously offer an originality that is not found in commercial tiles. The fact that each slab is made by hand gives every one slight irregularities in form, surface texture, and glaze. Original, one-of-a-kind designs on handpainted tiles can make for lively, representational murals, abstract geometric patterns, or more expressionist graphics. Add to this the fact that many contemporary ceramists approach their work through avenues of architecture, textile design, quilt making, painting, weaving, and sculpture, and it is readily apparent that there is a rich design diversity to be found in handmade tiles.

But despite their uniformity, commercial tiles can be installed with almost an equal amount of innovation. Dynamic and inventive surface patterns can be created by varying the color, shape, and size of tiles. Likewise, colored grouts can be used to highlight the grid of tiles, or to play off the colors used in the tiles themselves.

Finally, of course, is the possibility of using both handmade and commercial tiles in a single installation: A grid of uniform tiles may be interrupted with an inset of handpainted tiles.

But perhaps what is most striking about both kinds of tiles is their patterns. The customary square form of most tiles, when

A combination of checkerboard, solid, and diamond patterns in this tiled bathroom makes for lively geometric patterning that is somewhat more provocative than classic black-and-white checkerboard tiles. By drawing on a traditional tile application, then exaggerating its patterns, designer Andrée Putman demonstrates how tradition can be carried on in a contemporary manner.

assembled, makes for a grid pattern. And what is most appealing about this pattern is not how it is created, but how it is broken. The repetition that is in the very nature of tile work establishes a rhythm; how this rhythm is then continued and broken, established and shifted, gently or abruptly makes for a rich visual diversity.

Add to this the obvious fact that the tile actually need not be square at all, and the possibilities of pattern are nearly infinite. Parquet, staggered brick, checkerboard squares and squares on the diagonal, herringbone rectangles, and hexagonal stripes are only some of the more common patterns. Each of these patterns can be combined with others, or with handmade tiles of unique, one-of-a-kind proportions and shapes, testifying to the design diversity tile work offers.

Tiles, like stencils and several other forms of surface decoration, can be used to ornament an entire surface or to simply work as an accent on a border—to frame a window or door, for example, or to highlight a backsplash, or to climb the walls in a single decorative stripe. That they can be used in such a variety of ways further demonstrates their design versatility.

The ceramic tile reliefs by artist Nina Yankowitz work as architectural landscapes, left. She uses a variety of commercial, handmade, and hand-painted tiles in her one-of-a-kind installations. They often combine in a single project a regimented grid and pattern with less-restrained expressionist movements. What makes the work provocative is that order and disorder are evoked simultaneously.

Architect Alan Buchsbaum has used standard commercial wall tiles of different colors and sizes to create a mosaiclike effect for a bath. Soft grids of color blend into one another, demonstrating that soft, random color patterns can be as effective as the more structured patterns of color in more traditional applications.

Designer Joy Wulke has used small, two-inch standard commercial tiles for the intricate geometric patterning in the bathroom. The pastel peaches, lilacs, and blues as well as the minute dimensions of the tiles themselves give the design a delicacy and lightness that is not traditionally associated with the durability of tiles.

CHAPTER
5

WALLS OF GLASS

The intriguing aspects of designing surfaces with glass are shown in this expansive wall of glass block, which makes for a shimmering portal that opens to a three-story cylindrical vestibule. The translucent entryway in this private residence was designed by architects Thom Mayne and Michael Rotondi.

The rear wall of a New York City townhouse was reconstructed as a bay window to overlook a private garden and greater urban landscape. The wall of decoratively etched glass windows, with its Art Deco styling and a calla lily motif designed by Lynn Goodpasture, juxtaposes the urban view, which, of course, it partially obscures.

While there is ample speculation about the behavior of those living in glass houses, there is little question about the visual grace of its architectural applications. Interior walls, windows, and screens are only some of the surfaces in the home that invite treatment in glass, both traditional and modern. The various solutions found by craftsmen, architects, and designers range from leaded, etched, painted, and beveled glass to walls of glass blocks and to intriguing designs that combine all of these.

Architectural glass works as a veil between spaces. As such, it bends and alters light and color. It does not form so much as it transforms. While glass walls and partitions may work as physical barriers, the fact that they are translucent makes their effect slightly ambiguous. Herein lies the beauty and function. Rooms or hallways without windows can often benefit from glass walls separating them from areas with more light. Spaciousness, light, and openness can exist simultaneously with privacy in a room partially defined by a wall of glass blocks. A glass wall can both set apart and connect.

This inherent ambiguity is all the more evident when the glass has been manipulated in some way. Leaded glass, etched and sandblasted glass, beveled and cut glass are all decorative treatments that, while ornamenting the surface of the glass, also play with its opacity and translucence. In some cases the design on the glass panel and how it alters what appears through it is ornament enough in itself. Stripes of clear and sandblasted glass

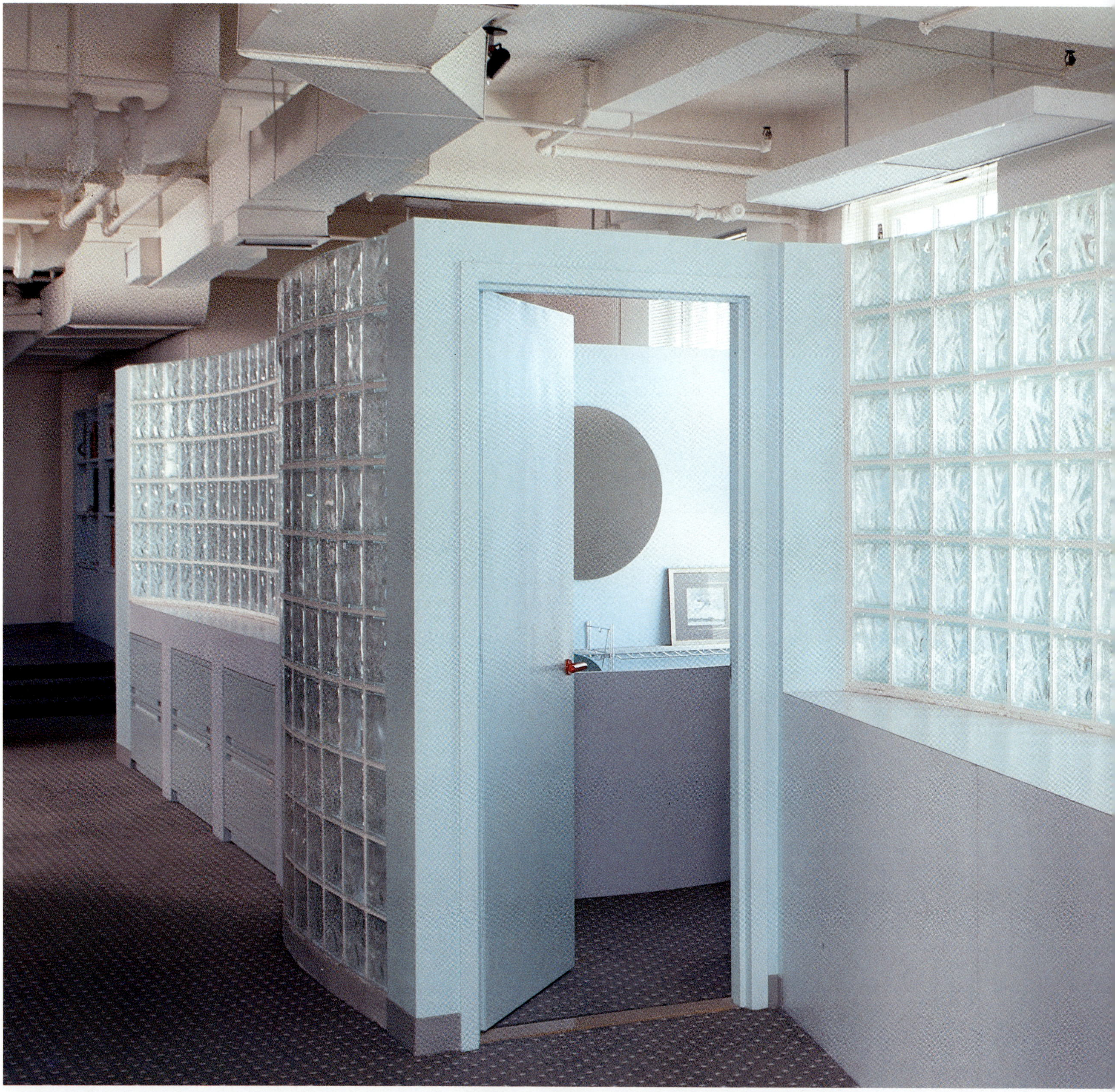

Architect Alan Buchsbaum has thrown a soft curve to the traditional grid of a glass block wall, above. The elliptical curves of glass permit light from windows on the east facing corridor to enter the work space on the other side of the wall. The combination of drywall with glass blocks nevertheless maintains the sense of privacy.

A curved wall comprised of glass blocks in a dining area designed by architect Brian Murphy allows natural light into the room while maintaining its sense of privacy, left. Likewise, the light from that area enters a kitchen area through a series of vertical cutouts in the wall, patterns of which align with the grid of glass blocks. Along with the tiled counter and floor, the entire space works as a series of grids that sometimes correspond to one another, sometimes contradict one another.

will, for example, devise their own provocative shapes while creating small mysteries of what lies behind.

In other cases, a surface of glass and its decorative patterns, such as leading or the varied textures of glass blocks, will cast shadows, creating a three-dimensional effect. In both instances, the magic of the glass is due at least in part to graceful manipulations of light and color. Its gentle bending of natural sunlight or more dramatic coloring and shaping of artificial light demonstrates how a flat sheet can affect space in an atmospheric way. The patterns and designs glass panels can create will change as the level and quality of illumination shifts and adds to their design versatility. The inherent properties of glass and their effect on color, light, and shadow, indeed render it a two-dimensional building material that has a three-dimensional effect on space.

The interest and imagination found on glass surfaces of contemporary architecture also reflect the work of contemporary craftsmen who, while continuing the traditions of an ancient art, have also found more modern applications. Leaded glass, commonly known as "stained glass," is one technique, for example, that has invited renewed attention and new, innovative applications. Traditionally, lead lines have been structural, holding small, brightly colored pieces of glass in place. Contemporary craftsmen, however, tend to use the lead lines as a more emphatic graphic element in itself. By varying their width, they use lead lines to "draw" on the glass. Often, false lead lines are a part of the design—rather than structure—of the glass panel.

But such an application is only one instance of an ancient craft in contemporary application. And while craftsmen continue to draw, etch, shape, and sculpt glass, more and more designers are finding architectural applications for these pieces. While a glass wall may speak for its inhabitant's vulnerability, its subtle manipulations on light and color will ensure that it is a statement of grace and eloquence.

Both real and false lead lines compose the abstract patterns of glass artist Marni Bakst's leaded glass panels, right. Real lead lines are structural and connect to one another, while false lead lines—applied for aesthetic rather than structural reasons—have been "appliquéd" and can terminate on the glass. Bakst combines antique, or mouth-blown glass, with standard commercial glass.

A wall of etched glass permits northern light to penetrate and illuminate an otherwise dark entrance and atrium designed by architect Henry Smith-Miller, left. The grid plays with opacity and translucence, and its thin lines are repeated in the living area behind it. The austere lines of the grid are reinforced and juxtaposed by angles of a bright red railing. A small interior window frames the view of the two-story atrium and captures its concise and serene geometrics.

Glass artist Marni Bakst has used both antique leaded and sandblasted glass for an interior bay wall which is backlit with fluorescent light. The sweeping lines of the abstract design give the panels a sense of movement not ordinarily associated with the tranquil still life compositions found in traditional leaded glass work.

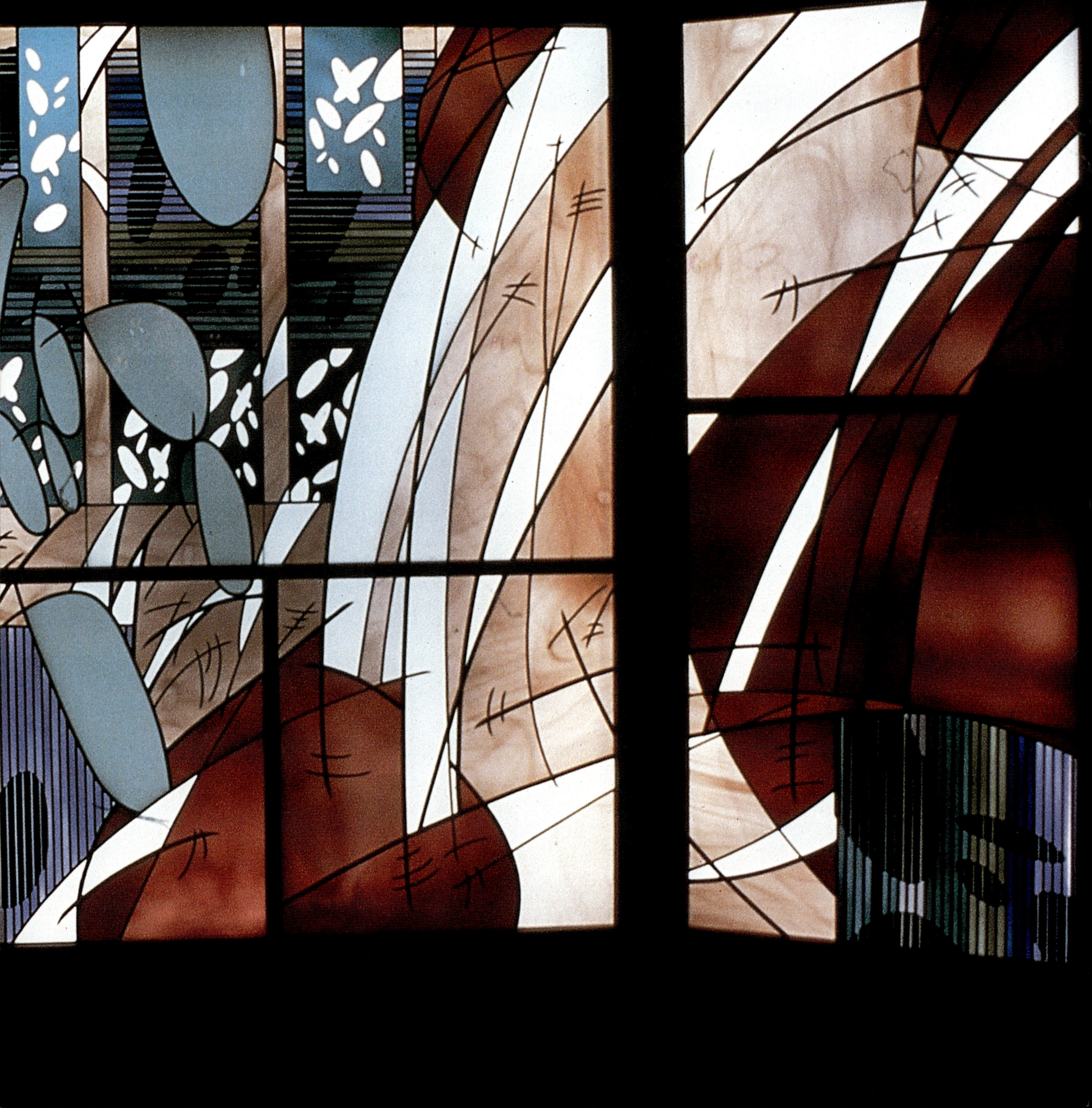

CHAPTER
6

WALLPAPERS AND FABRICS

Wallpaper often takes on the form of art, as shown in "Heavy Texture," a handpainted wallcovering by Art People. Overlapping colors work to create a three-dimensional effect; seemingly random strokes of a matte top layer are applied over a bottom multicolored layer of more translucent colors. The lustre of the surfaces plays with light while their texture creates a sculptural effect.

The movements of the painter's hand remain evident in "Salina"—a hand-painted, iridescent wallcovering by Art People, right. Using a paint that is resin based with pigment, the designers have created a tactile, impasto surface. The elasticity of the paint is such that the fabric can be used to wrap around columns or other architectural details without chipping or cracking its surface.

The continuous zigzag ridges of "Herringbone" by Art People repeat themselves every eight inches in matte or iridescent finishes, left.

The design tradition of applying printed paper to the wall is long and rooted in many cultures. Papers depicting religious figures, for example, were used in the Middle Ages to conceal cracks in the wall. It was not until the seventeenth century, however, that the practice became more purposeful and stylized when stenciled and painted papers and fabrics were applied to walls as less costly imitations of the woven tapestries and rich brocades used by the artistocracy.

Since then, of course, wallpapers and fabrics have become a less imitative art with a design history and aesthetic of their own. Dominotiers, a guild of painters and papermakers in sixteenth-century France, produced domino papers, simple, handcolored, geometric stenciled designs used to line books, boxes, and trunks, in addition to walls. These simple patterns gave way in the eighteenth century to elaborate floral designs and rich landscapes; with the opening of trade routes to the Orient came more exotic landscapes and imagery. By the end of the eighteenth century, wallpaper had become a major element of interior design, as was demonstrated by its opulence and complexity. Cylinder printing in the nineteenth century facilitated its production and coloration, as was demonstrated by patterns that could include precise geometrics, stylized floral arrangements, and subtle landscapes all in a single design.

As the technology of printing developed, so too did the

complexity of designs found on wallpapers. Entire panoramic murals could be reproduced in a wide, subtle color palette. Wallpaper design also frequently patterned itself on architecture, duplicating on a two-dimensional surface friezes, moldings, pilasters, brickwork, marble, and wood.

Not surprisingly, by the end of the nineteenth century, more restrained geometrics were again in favor. The opulence and often dazzling clutter of Victorian design had reached a surfeit, a period of design excess that gave rise to the Arts and Crafts Movement. Generated by William Morris, the movement encouraged a more naturalistic approach to design and decoration. The simplicity of line and form in Morris's design in general, and wallpaper in particular, found an appreciative audience, and his simple woodblock papers, sensitive to color, texture, and form, were widely used.

The design of wallpapers and fabrics in the years that followed has continued to reflect trends in fashion and art, rather than establishing them. Fractured leaves and abstract petals found in patterns of the twenties were not unrelated to Cubist painting, and the designs of both Picasso and Matisse found their way to wallpaper as well as to canvas. Similarly, in more recent times, the supergraphics of the 1960s appeared on wallpaper too, and both Andy Warhol and Saul Steinberg have lent designs developed on canvas to wallpaper.

Nevertheless, the use of wallpaper and fabrics as surface decoration declined during the age of Modernism, which put forth the decree that surface ornament was not unlike crime, and it has not been until more recent times that wallpaper has again become an acceptable design option. With the interest in minimalist design fading, and with the renewed appreciation for ornamentation, wallpaper and fabric have enjoyed renewed favor.

And as such, designers and architects have rediscovered the appeal of paper and fabric surfaces as a way to bring decoration and color to expansive surfaces without laborious handpainting or even stenciling. But aside from their sheer ornamentation, patterned wallpapers can also have a visual effect on the shape or size of a room. Thin, vertical stripes, for example, can add height to a room with a low ceiling; likewise, a strong pattern can set certain areas apart or act as a backdrop for specific pieces of furniture.

It is not the design elements of wallpaper alone, however, that make it an appealing surface material. The process of Scotchgarding protects fabrics from moisture, stains, and normal wear and tear. Likewise, washable vinyls available on the market today are both durable and easy to maintain. Finally, the development of flame-retardant wallcoverings offers obvious advantages. Finishes vary as well, from flat to matte to gloss finishes, and the combination of these on a single design

Neo-Grec patterns by Bradbury & Bradbury with coordinating wall and ceiling elements include four Greek maidens depicting the four elements— air, earth, fire, and water. These ceiling elements are all individual modular patterns that can be used separately or in many different combinations.

can make for a play with light and surface. Add to this the availability of metallic or Mylar papers—developed first by NASA through research on protective coverings—and the play with light and reflection can become all the more dramatic. Fabrics and wallpapers are no longer simply fragile surfacing materials, and it is the quality of the materials as well as their decorative attributes that give them their special appeal.

The contemporary market offers a wide range of wallpapers and fabrics. There are precise reproduction patterns of Victorian florals, William Morris designs, or stylized Art Nouveau and Art Deco patterns. There are also contemporary designs marked by more random patterns, designs that are less mathematical;

Random, intersecting, pastel lines compose the iridescent geometric patterning of "Beams," a wallcovering from Groundworks, left. Both its design and its glimmering surface-play with light mark it a contemporary wall treatment.

"Myrtle" and "Iris," shown on pages 80 and 81, are wallpapers originally designed by William Morris, designer, craftsman, poet, painter, essayist, and founder of the nineteenth-century Arts and Crafts Movement in England. Morris's reverence for natural form and color are reflected a century later in the stylized floral patterns and vibrant hues of the papers reproduced by Scalamandré. Thick foliage works as a background for the intertwining and patterning of blossoms, stalks, and leaves.

By combining a delicate floral lily motif against a stronger geometric pattern, "Baroque" by China Seas continues a long stylistic tradition of wallpaper design, left.

Fabric designer Inger McCabe Elliott has drawn on the ancient textile art of Javanese batik in designing collections of wallcoverings for China Seas. "Batavia," right, is one of these designs. It is clearly influenced by the brilliant colors and imagery of the traditional Indonesian folk art.

VICTORIAN FLORALS

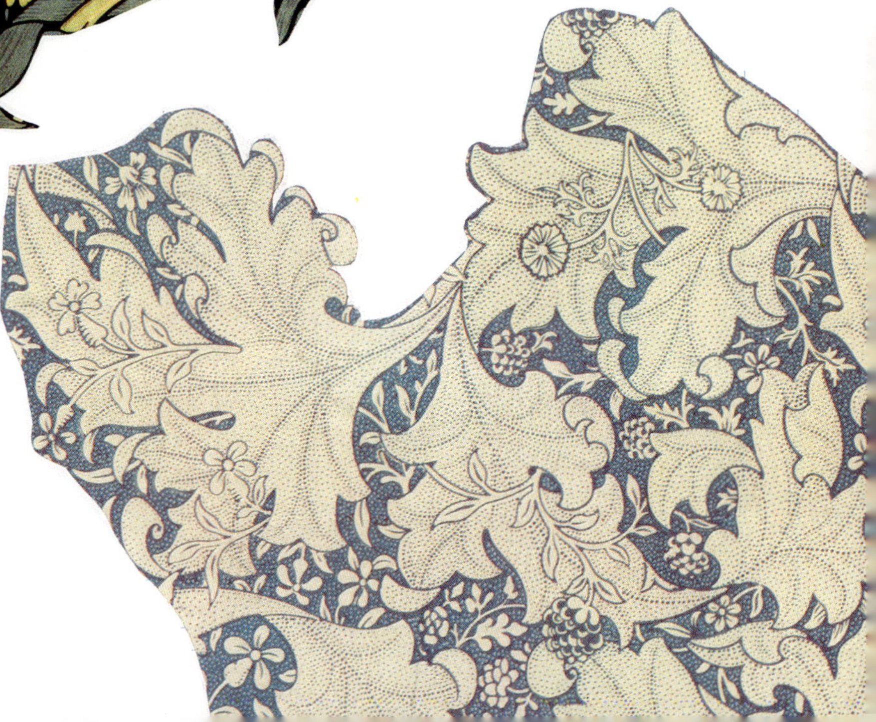

Wallpaper patterns by Bradbury & Bradbury with an Anglo-Japanese flavor are featured in this parlor in Baltimore's Government House, which was restored by the design firm of Johnson/Berman. A Renaissance Revival settee and side chairs in red silk damask complement the hand silk-screened wallpapers, opposite.

Last year the Baltimore-based design firm of Johnson/Berman restored an 1889 building in Baltimore known as Government House. In this parlor Neo-Grec wallpapers by Bradbury & Bradbury add a true sense of elegance and style, right.

repeats less precise. Patterns are established only to be broken. Geometric shapes are scattered across a surface in a seemingly accidental arrangement. These designs are less regimented, more spontaneous. Offered too, in blatant revolt against the luxury and rich texture of many historical wallpapers, are those that simply resemble brown paper bags.

Also available are handpainted wallpapers with patterns and designs that are altogether distinguished by the picturesque irregularities of handwork. Fabrics and papers can be lush and marblized or spotted, sprayed, spattered, splashed, and squeegeed for a tactile effect. While many of these fabrics and papers may appear to have the random splashes of a painter's dropcloth, their patterns have actually been standardized, do in fact, repeat, and are in the end, reproducible. It is only in their unusual appearance that their individual textures and designs rebel against the tradition of precise and discernible repetitions that identifies the majority of wallpapers.

Coco Chanel, the renowned French couturier, sheathed her dressing room walls and ceiling in black oil cloth to create dark, shimmering surfaces that appeared to have a depth all their own. Even fabrics such as this, without any surface pattern or variation whatsoever, can make for striking surface treatment. And as the inventive use of oil cloth suggests, it may be the application rather than the material that makes for an innovative surface. But whether it is a question of imagination in application or material, or both, it is clear that the age-old design practice of using fabric and paper as an interior surfacing material is bringing new pleasure to today's walls.

bayer

CHAPTER
7

TAPESTRIES AND WALLHANGINGS

Wallhangings can often be grouped in the same family with painted canvases, but they are distant cousins. "Progressions Once Reversed," designed by Herbert Bayer and produced by Modern Master Tapestries, is a case in point. Says Bayer, "The natural dye of the yarn results in a richness and depth of color which is impossible to obtain with painted pigment."

Tapestries have been used for architectural as well as decorative purposes throughout the ages. In Medieval times, their purpose was to diminish the draft in huge stone halls. While there might not be any direct analogy between these and the towering corporate headquarters of contemporary times where immense wallhangings are often found today, they definitely lend a similar warmth to oversize space. Tapestries are just as applicable in the home; although residential spaces may be built on a more intimate scale, they are as accommodating to the warm colors and soft lines of handwoven textiles.

The pictorial images found on Medieval tapestries reflected religious allegory and symbolism integral to life in the Middle Ages. Likewise, those found in contemporary tapestries express today's culture. The unrestrained color and spontaneous design of expressionist painting translate clearly from canvas to woven textile, though perhaps with more volume and texture; and the depth of color that can be achieved through natural dyes may result in paintings in fiber that are expressive more than narrative. Likewise, the abstract use of color and pattern explored by many contemporary painters and sculptors is part of a long tradition in handwoven textiles. The most prominent examples are those made by the Navajo Indians.

"Amerind Landscape" by Roy Lichtenstein and Modern Master Tapestries, left, demonstrates how images in contemporary art can be translated from one medium to another—in this case from pop, comic-book graphics, to the painted canvas, to tapestry.

"Personage & Animal" designed by Karen Appel, right, has been rendered in wool in an edition of ten by Modern Master Tapestries, Inc.

The limited editions produced by Modern Master Tapestries are developed through a collaborative process with artist and artisan. While tapestries are woven individually by artisans in India or France, the artist is involved in all stages of production from the choice of materials, to the selection of weaving technique, to the final approval of each finished piece. "Color is a tactile result in tapestry, since it is woven," says painter Ken Noland. And indeed, tapestries of Noland's targets and stripes translate the subtle colors of his work to a more textural surface, right.

Cynthia Schira's tapestry, "The Kingdom of Wu," opposite page, is a field painting in textile. A subdued landscape, its gradations of color evoke open horizons, scattered light, a wash of shadow. Her subtle palette of colors and patterns are soft departures from the traditional clear confines of the grid, the repetitive designs predicated by the loom. Despite the artistic effect, however, Schira's work is produced on a computerized loom which simultaneously makes available a greater number of weave constructions than can be done by hand.

Just as traditional tapestries were often a textile translation of painting and murals, contemporary pieces may be based on photographs. Such is the case with the work of the Scheuer Tapestry Studio. Although Ruth Scheuer works in a studio not unlike those of her medieval predecessors, with apprentices who exchange time for training, she also works from color slides and photographs to reproduce modern landscapes. This rendition of the Queensborough Bridge in New York City, woven at Scheuer Tapestry Studio by Susan Minnich and Deborah Hildreth, right, is indeed contemporary, but reproduced in an age-old medium.

Similarly, the play with pattern that is evident in contemporary decorative arts finds an ideal medium in the grid of the woven surface. Patterns are defined by warp and weft, only to be softly broken and disrupted. Geometrics are established only to be subtly shifted, turned on their sides, gone askew. And tapestries can be representational too, drawing on the contemporary style of photo-realism. These, however, tend to draw more upon urban imagery than the pastoral landscapes of their predecessors. This is one of the beauties of the medium. Historically, tapestries and wallhangings have drawn upon their own rich design traditions as well as on those of other mediums; contemporary pieces do as well. Tapestries work as a design tradition in themselves and as a mirror that reflects the other artistic idioms of the culture they are derived from.

But imagery and subject matter are not the only ways in which contemporary tapestries reflect their time. Their designs also reflect recent graphic technologies. Photography and photo silkscreening, for example, both happily translate to the woven surface. Computer graphics also have a place in textile arts, where programmed sequences of pattern and color and their pictorial deviations are put onto fabric.

The work of contemporary craftsmen is marked by the degree to which it observes the traditions of the art, and to the degree it departs from them entirely. Some artists adhere to the traditional grid, but use synthetic materials such as metallic threads, nylon monofilaments, polyethylene twines, or rubber

Kris Dey's textural wall panels are not woven, but rather, are constructed of torn cotton strips wrapped around lightweight plastic tubing. The tubes are then strung together. The fabric has been painted with textile paints in carefully planned sequences, making for a surface that appears to have light shimmering across it.

tubing. Or often, such materials may be used in conjunction—and contrast—with natural materials such as wool, linen, silk, or cotton threads, or even sisal, hemp, goathair, and horsehair.

Other artists alter the traditional rectangular shape of the wallhanging, curving it, twisting it, distorting it. Random geometrics as well as sensuous, rounded forms deviate from the often austere confines established by the conventional grid of the loom.

And other artisans have shaped textile constructions that come off the wall completely to enter the realm of sculpture. The traditional flat weave of much textile art has yielded to experimentation with knotting, knitting, appliqué, and felting in tactile constructions that are often three-dimensional.

Yet with all this play and experimentation in fiber arts, it is often easy to lose sight of the fact that such pieces can and do serve a function. While tapestries are obviously not structural, they can have a more subtle, but very real, effect on space. Hung from the ceiling they can work as screens to visually, rather than structurally, create and divide space. And like screens, bright colors and strong shapes will emphatically define space, while paler, more translucent textiles will simply suggest it.

But tapestries and wallhangings also have an acoustical effect on space that add to their appeal. Woven materials will tend to absorb or muffle sound, thereby softening it. And just as they absorb sound, they can also work as insulation in extreme temperatures, warm or cold.

Finally, the symbolic warmth and color of handcrafted textiles must be considered. In the austere architecture of Modernism, the deep colors and tactile surfaces of a tapestry can imbue the space with a warmth, even sensuousness, that might otherwise be lacking. In architecture dominated by steel, glass, and masonry, a handwoven wallhanging indeed brings a more human sense of workmanship. Fiber arts bring a softness to hard edges; a wash of warmth and color to neutral areas; and a brief landscape of beautiful handwork to the space, surface, and structure of the home.

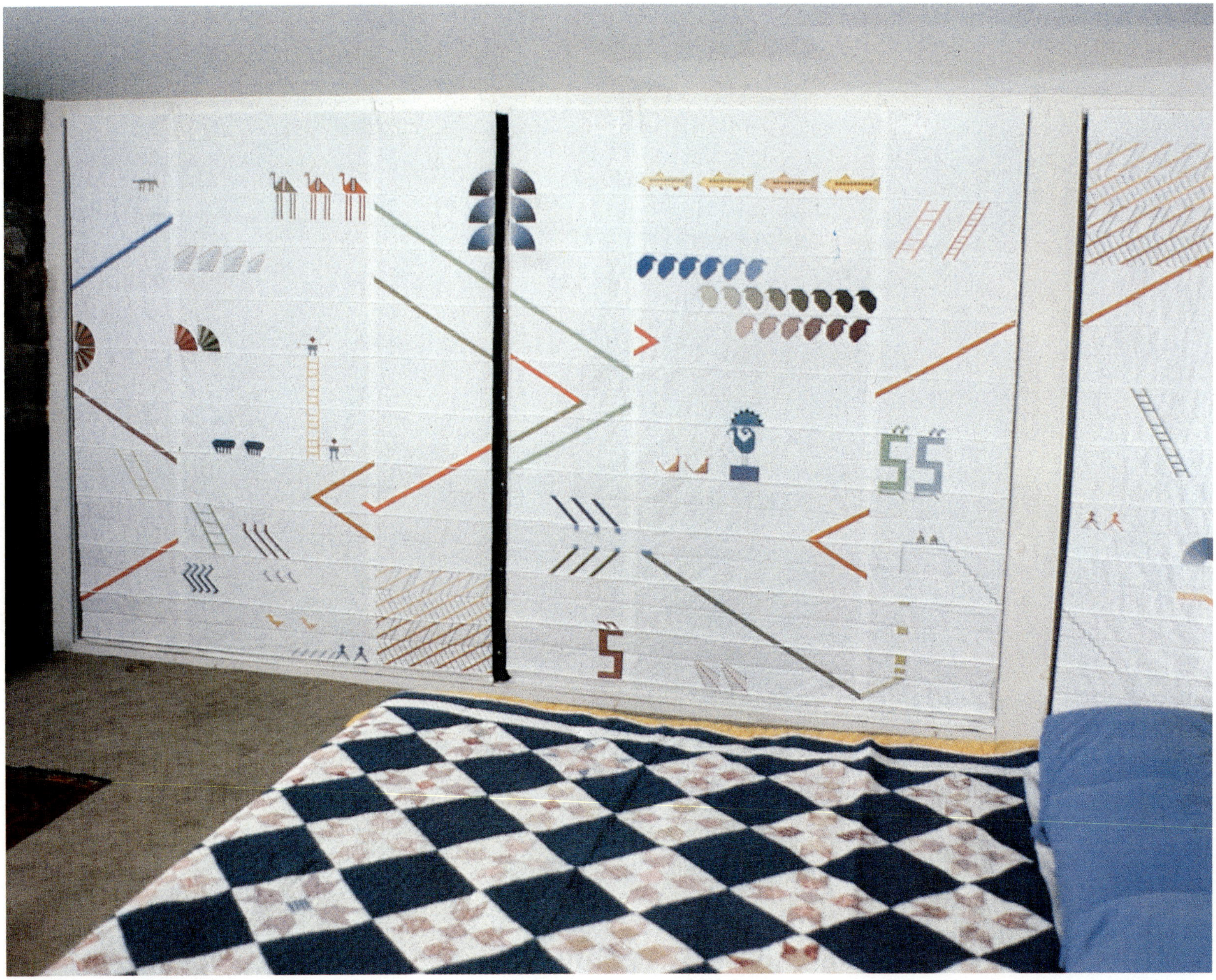

"Folding Menagerie," above, by Anne McKenzie Nickolson works as a covering for a bedroom window, with three appliquéd and embroidered cotton panels that fold down to let in additional light. Images are both geometric and random. Nickolson's clients had a collection of tapestries and oriental rugs; "they were always looking for the animals in them," says Nickolson, "so I tried to suggest similar motifs in my work."

Satin ribbon that has been sewn onto strips of cotton, which are then sewn together, construct "Dancing Diagonals" by Anne McKenzie Nickolson, right. The rich, electric patterning of the wall piece corresponds both to the patterning of the carpet and the neon sign also hanging on the wall.

CHAPTER
8

ARCHITECTURAL SCREENS

Screens have the power to create a sense of mystery, as shown in this one by architect and designer Preston Phillips, which uses a grid of clear and sandblasted glass. Its alternating transparence and translucence makes for provocative visual play of the objects behind the screen and the shadows they create.

A partition of glass blocks has been used by architect Rebecca Binder in a plan to separate dining area from living room, right. While the "screen" is only partial height and quite transparent, its soft curve nevertheless suggests a visual separation between the two areas.

The one-of-a-kind and limited edition, handmade, folding screens designed and produced by C/W Studios are constructed with fine hardwoods and subtle ikat silks. Panels are reversible: On this screen, left, one side is a silk ikat, woven and dyed in soft tones; on the other, walnut rubbed with clear satin lacquer. Weaver and textile designer Catherine Creamer uses the computer in designing her fabrics, finding that computer graphics enable her to develop weaves that compliment the surface patterns of wood. "After a thorough development on computer," she explains, "I can choose designs that echo the richness of birdseye maple or the lustre of satinwood."

The use of screens as an architectural device has considerable historical precedence. In fourth-century China, painted partitions of silk and paper were used as pictorial rather than structural wall panels. In sixth- and seventh-century Japan, the architectural panels became mobile, serving as interior sliding walls that could be erected quickly and simply. Their series of folded images, moreover, worked as a graphic narrative, revealing royal histories, tales, and heroic myths. As a self-supporting, temporary partition, the screen was a decorative and efficient way to structure and restructure space.

In more recent years, artists, architects, and craftsmen have rediscovered and worked to refine an ancient tradition, finding that the folding screen meets a number of quite contemporary needs. In dense urban areas, especially where acoustical privacy is near impossible, visual privacy, all the more prized, can be achieved by screens; where privacy is often a feat of the imagination, the screen can do much to boost it. In a city environment where privacy and spaciousness are both valued commodities, the screen, as a room divider, is often the architectural device that can serve both purposes. As a temporary partition, the screen acknowledges the need for open space; nevertheless, its efficiency in structuring and dividing space permits occasional solitude without the need for costly permanent architectural changes.

The folding screen is a way of achieving instant architecture, which is no doubt the reason for its current appeal. Screens, despite their often provocative graphics, are no-commitment architecture. In a culture that prizes instant results, their efficiency in appearing and disappearing is of great value.

The merit of the screen does not lie simply in its practicality. At once flat and three-dimensional, its images and forms can appear as both painted and sculptural. But rarely does one

Architectural Screen™ by Gretchen Bellinger Inc is a woven stainless steel fabric ideal for interior screens, ceiling and wall panels, and room dividers. Its fine weave allows for a soft, shimmering translucence while its metallic threads have their own reflective lustre and color. The screen has been used in this residence, above, designed by Mies van der Rohe and updated by Powell/Kleinschmidt to conceal the doors of a storage wall, a design that allows the unit to work as a subtle space divider rather than a storage unit.

The silk-covered panels used in Jack Lenor Larsen's New York loft, designed in collaboration with Charles Forberg, act as temporary partitions for the expansive loft space, right. Similarly, when opened, some panels reveal Larsen's extensive glass, porcelain, and ceramic collection; other panels work as window coverings that softly filter natural light. The forty panels, based on traditional Japanese shoji (transparent sliding screens) and fusama (opaque sliding screens), glide easily along exposed tracks.

When painter and fabric designer Katherine Cheney Humpstone found she needed to partition space in her own loft, her logical solution was to bring her own canvases off the wall. One subsequent screen she designed was acrylic and oil stick on canvas stretched across a poplar frame; on another, she used acrylic paints directly on birch veneer, right. Two-way hinges add to the flexibility of the screens, while different designs on either side of the panels allow the screens to be all the more effective as space dividers.

Ambiguous and evocative, the images painted on Jack Radetsky's screens appear as shadows created by objects and light behind the screen, left. Radetsky chose to use the three-dimensional screen for his images as a means with which to extend the atmosphere of his paintings into the environment. Indeed, the illusions, shadows, and light of his images make for provocative visual play and puzzling questions about what is on the screen and what is behind.

find in the folds of the contemporary screens the narratives of their historical antecedents. Rather, the graphic texture and sculptural shape of many screens qualify them literally and figuratively as off-the-wall art. Many craftsmen, painters, and sculptors who design these screens admit that it was the expressionist canvases stretched across the wooden stretchers of their earlier paintings that led to experimentation with larger pieces that might work architecturally or with the environment. Indeed, the three-dimensional folds of the screen often allow it to create total environments. Add to this the fact that the panels have two visible sides as well as a myriad of angles, curves, and folds that are mobile, and the possibilities multiply. Clearly, the utilitarian nature of the screen does not in any way at all prevent it from being a dramatic piece of art.

Whether a screen works in the environment as a practical, movable wall, a piece of sculpture, a free-standing painting, a piece of furniture, or all of these, it is an implicit, rather than explicit, way of maneuvering space. Screens work as walls visually rather than structurally. Nevertheless, the materials used in construction are what will finally determine the effect; the color, surface, and texture of the panels will determine how different screens play with space. Because they let in light, glass screens—sandblasted or etched—may simply be an elusive suggestion of a partition. Likewise, paper and fabric screens that don't completely block out whatever is on the other side of them may suggest separation rather than really provide for

Despite their icy color, the oversized tropical leaves and flora of environmental artist and sculptor Pat Norvell's screens create a veritable glass jungle. Sandblasted onto glass panels, the images recall Art Nouveau motifs which become all the more effective since the form of the panels follows the outlines of the gigantic leaves, petals, and tendrils.

it. Alternatively, the more substantial material of wooden screens, and the bright colors and strong shapes of their painted decorations, can more emphatically divide space.

Both architectural and decorative, screens are a flexible means with which to structure space. Even the depth of the fold allows for variations in the amount of space it occupies. And screens often have an even more practical function; they are able to conceal an unsightly air-conditioning unit, for example, or eliminate dead space.

The folded screen can be a graceful, movable balance between decoration and function, between art and furniture. The art and the industry, the skill and the ingenuity apparent in contemporary handmade screens point out how this temporary architecture can indeed have a more lasting effect.

Designed by Louise Crandell for Serpentine Studio, this screen, right, has been constructed in plywood and painted in oil and metallic paints. Its eight-panel form exploits the traditional folds and angles of the screen. Jagged geometrics and the play with dark and light give the panels more dramatic turns, twists, and edges. That one side of the screen is pale and the other darker gives it a greater flexibility. The linear design, with its enigmatic perspectives, is indeed architectural, while the points and pinnacles of the screen's crest is not unlike a postmodern urban skyline.

Arlene Slavin's vivid animals, fish, and birds—built and painted on a human scale—evoke both a primitive and sensuous environment, left and opposite page. Images of pelicans, herons, exotic tropical fish, antelope, and oversized birds are painted on both sides of the plywood screens; cutout silhouettes of flora and fauna, while letting light through, also give further dimension to the screen.

CHAPTER
9

WORKING WALLS

Beauty and function combine in these symmetrical stacks of white oak cabinets. They are punctuated with rounded black rubber pulls in an arrangement that demonstrates how fixtures can work as strong design accents. The cabinets line a dressing-room corridor designed by Thom Mayne and Michael Rotondi.

In a shelving unit designed for a Manhattan loft, above, architect Alan Buchsbaum has exploited the asymmetrical. Shelves of different woods, varied textures, grains, colors, widths, and proportions have been combined in one wall unit. To the right, open shelving, glass windows, and standard wooden doors all add up to an eclectic and visually lively plan in these kitchen cabinets designed by architect Alan Buchsbaum. Porcelain knobs do not line up nor do shelves center with one another.

While most people are likely to think of their walls as either structural devices intended to support a ceiling or roof or the means by which different areas of the home might be divided, most designers and architects think otherwise. Those in urban areas—where usable space is often at a premium—are attuned to the fact that walls may serve myriad other purposes.

But it is not simply the urban plight of space shortage that creates the need for working walls. For professionals anywhere who opt to work from their homes, the practical requirements of office or studio space will often demand that walls serve several functions at once; storing materials and equipment in an accessible and orderly system; supporting shelving and work counters; or providing for seating.

Likewise, collectors of paintings, sculpture, porcelain, ceramics, or even books and records will also opt for walls that serve double duty, walls that can be used to exhibit or simply store their extensive collections.

While such walls continue to serve their traditional and

Design consultant Michael Haskins devised this grid of shelving units for a bedroom, below. While the grid of shelves itself has been constructed of white Formica® Colorcore®, the backing on each unit is a different shade from the Colorcore® pastel palette. The gentle play with color softens the otherwise hard lines of the grid, which also permits the shelves to function both as areas for storage and as display units.

Green Plexiglas battens with painted edges have been mounted with metal acorn nuts to make for decorative detailing on a wall treatment by the architectural firm A2Z, left and above. Titled "Facadomy," the unit was designed to ornament an otherwise uninteresting cabinet unit.

The wall niche above, designed by architect Lee Skolnick, takes the idea of the traditional window seat to playful extremes. The wood niche, painted a deep gray, has been inset into a double brick wall, with the small square window punched through both layers of brick. The niche provides both shelving above and a bench for seating below.

In a private residence designed by architect Charles Moore, rows of uniform, built-in kitchen cabinets line up in a wall of elegant symmetry, right. Their neat repetition of rows and their vertical white planking make for a simplicity that recalls the efficiency and purity of Shaker design.

obvious purposes, they can also be put to work as storage spaces, display areas, and multi-level shelving. Working walls can conceal appliances and electronic gear; or they can display them in practical and attractive arrangements. The purposes they may serve are only as limited as the imagination of their designers.

But practicality need not be at the expense of design. Storage units can have a decorative appeal; symmetry or the intended lack of it in open shelving can make for its own style; sculptural fixtures, knobs, and handles can accent what might otherwise be a tedium of cabinets or shelves; or the innovative use of material can distract one from the mundane function it serves.

The wit and artistry in design solutions are often in direct proportion to the challenge of the design. This being the case, walls that need to serve more than one purpose invite innovation.

CHAPTER 10

EXTERIOR WALLS

A striking exterior wall leading to a poolhouse has been painted by architect Charles Moore in the bright supergraphics favored in the 1960s. Its brilliant colors and target pattern are in vivid, visual contrast to both the natural wood flooring and rough concrete walls surrounding it.

A blue-green latticework of walls brings an unexpected garden atmosphere to the blacktop geography of an urban rooftop terrace designed by architects Rodolfo Machado and Jorge Silvetti. Aside from its evocations of a rural summerhouse, however, the lattice is also a way of permitting transparency while defining separate "rooms."

Most exterior walls, by their nature, are not intended so much to provide shelter but to set apart usable exterior space. Not necessarily attached to roofs nor necessarily with any real structural value, they are less bound by function than interior walls. In many cases they do not define space so much as they suggest it; function, too, is merely alluded to. As markers in open spaces, exterior walls punctuate this sense of openness. Walls of lattice, open grids and frames, freestanding, sculptural stonework and all can be used very effectively to retain the sense of openness, if not outright exploit it.

Although the materials and finishes used to build exterior walls must be durable and weatherproof, it is not necessarily dictated that they appear so. Fragile latticework is as common to garden architecture as more solid stone and masonry. However, the choice of materials is largely determined by the climatic conditions prevailing at the construction site. In areas with extreme temperatures or temperature shifts, frequent precipitation, or strong winds, careful consideration of these factors should be made before selecting an exterior wall material.

The design of an exterior wall may be suggested, or actually determined, by the design of the structure it accompanies. The exterior walls of Frank Lloyd Wright's Storer house are a case in point, where the varying patterns of masonry blocks are used indoors and out to create a strong, continuous, visual

The sharp relief patterns in the 12-inch square masonry blocks of Frank Lloyd Wright's Storer house repeat themselves in different variations indoors and out. The texture of the blocks establishes a visual image that becomes more pronounced with the patterning of leaves and their shadows. Among Wright's legacies to contemporary architecture was his "organic" approach, which worked to fuse building with site. Such a fusion is clearly evident in both the interior and exterior of the Storer House.

The multilevel terraces designed by the Chicago firm Murphy/Jahn, left and right, are delineated by white lattice grids. The dimensions of the lattice panels reflect the solid panels used for interior space. The "outdoors" nature of the exterior stairway is emphasized by the open framework, which repeats the grid motif. The play with interior and exterior space, and how these are signaled with blanks and solids, brings the house to life.

rhythm. But it is not always necessary to create a visual connection between exterior walls and the design of the house or other central structure. It may be appropriate in some cases and, depending on intention, not in others.

More to the point in the design and construction of exterior walls is how they relate to their immediate outdoor environment. It is not just in function and material that exterior walls differ from interior walls. Their entire construction tends to be based more on their surroundings, be it woods and fields or a landscape of urban blacktop. Their purpose is more than simply to separate one room from another, but to set apart a useable, human space in an outdoor area. Often they must evoke a sense of retreat, so their design must in some way complement the specifics of their environs. Sometimes it does so by reflecting the rough surfaces and earth tones found in nature. But the design could just as well be bold in contrast. Or if the landscape is urban, the set of references will, of course, change.

In constructing exterior walls, the architect or designer is presented with a set of references that are outside of his or her aesthetic jurisdiction. While there are no hard and fast rules, he or she must start by acknowledging this fact. And there are as many varied solutions as there are landscapes.

CHAPTER
11

ONE▪OF▪A▪KIND WALLS

A unique wall is formed by pressed tin, a material conventionally found on warehouse ceilings. By applying the tin to the walls of a residential loft, architect and designer Preston Phillips has capitalized on its metallic sheen, its capacity to reflect light, and the ornamental form of its geometric grid.

Artist Dan Friedman is also a sculptor and graphic designer—skills he has clearly put to use in his own residence, right. Disparate images, colors, and forms collide with one another and then settle into their own baroque, graphic rhythm. Clearly such applications only begin on the wall, and more often than not end up completely off the wall.

A hall of mirrors creates its own play with space and surface, above. The spatial enigmas are framed in gold leaf and make for an elegance that is nevertheless disquieting. As a portrait gallery that reflects only itself, it suggests how a repetition of mirrors can make a provocative interior.

A simple wall of concrete blocks designed by architects Batey & Mack indicates how the usual becomes the unusual, right. Both the neat layering of the blocks and the clean lines of the mortar make for a cool balance and a symmetry that ties in to the grid of a tile floor and the block furniture. But it is the line of the scythe poised in this tableau of grids that throws a curve and softens the straight edges of the interior.

As is amply evident, surfaces can be painted, printed, and papered with a variety of textures and patterns, real or imagined. Ceramic tiles, glass, paper, fabric, wood, and woven textiles are all materials that can bring color and texture to the wall, permanent or impermanent. The following pages show applications that are less easy to categorize.

These are one-of-a-kind walls, unique for their applications of material or objects. Some of these use commonplace building materials—sheetrock, concrete block, pressed tin. Others use more unusual and extravagant materials. The point, however, is that it is the creative use of material, rather than simply the material itself, that finally makes for such startling and

This atmospheric dining area, right, was designed by Morsa for a single evening. The designers draped transparent white muslin from a twenty-eight-foot ceiling to create soft, billowing walls. The chairs and a fourteenth-century refractory table were likewise wrapped in muslin, evoking a summerhouse at the end of the season, when the furniture is draped in cloth and hidden. Champagne glasses were sandblasted white, as were forks and knives. Labels were removed from bottles, and those were frosted.

"At Home with Ghosts" is the way one magazine titled its story on this project by SITE, the innovative New York architectural firm known for its high-risk design solutions. And indeed, images and artifacts emerge mysteriously from the surface of the walls as though they were gentle visitations from a past era, below. The images are two-fold; some refer to architecture and furnishings of the 1820s, the period of the three-story Greek Revival house. Others are more private, based on the owner's personal history. The architects call it "built-in historical layering" and in fact, the gilt mirrors, ornate mantels, and candlesticks extend the spirit of the house.

Los Angeles artist and designer Peter Shire used an exotic assortment of handmade tiles for a small bathroom shown on these two pages. Shire cut the tiles as they were being installed in an improvisational and spontaneous arrangement. The sense of impulsiveness lingers, not only in the irregular shapes of the tiles but also in the random streaks of the handpainted glazes used on the blue tilework. Shire has taken ceramic bath tile to a new dimension quite literally, with pyramid and sphere-shaped tiles installed in the corner. With a Formica® Colorcore® sink and cabinet units and pink walls, Shire has used all the surfaces of the room as his canvas.

imaginative and impressive special effects.

Some, such as the dining room wrapped in muslin for a single evening's event, are clearly temporary arrangements. Others are more permanent. Pressed tin, a material that is conventionally found on warehouse ceilings, is highly reflective and can be as ornamental as more precious metals when it is applied to walls. Historical layering that emerges mysteriously from the walls of another house literally and figuratively extends the spirit of the home; the images and artifacts give an ordinary room an element of fantasy. Another treatment features a collection of mirrors of different sizes which reflect upon each other and create rooms within rooms, each with a whole new set of perspectives. One-of-a-kind arrangements of neatly layered blocks or an exotic composition of irregularly shaped handmade tiles like the ones shown here can be visually provocative, and are not easily forgotten. Innovative design solutions can emerge when we take the familiar, twist it, turn it around, and see it through new eyes.

While projects such as those shown may be difficult to duplicate, what they tell us is that there are few limits in design for those willing to take such chances.

APPENDIX

SOURCES
AMERICAN

ARCHITECTS AND DESIGNERS

A2Z
Box 351389
Los Angeles, CA 90035
213•937•207

BAM CONSTRUCTION AND DESIGN
1422 Second Street
Santa Monica, CA 90401
310•393•3252

MACK
246 First Street
San Francisco, CA 94105
415•777•5305

GINA BEADLE
Box 571
Amagansett, NY 11930
516•267•3017

THOMAS H. BEEBY & KIRTSEN PELTZER BEEBY
Hammond Beeby and Babka Inc.
440 North Wells Street
Chicago, Il 60610
312•527•3200

REBECCA BINDER, FAIA
7726 81 Street
Playa Del Rey, CA 90293
310•301•0260

SAM BOTERO, ASSOCIATES
150 East 58 Street
New York, NY 10155
212•935•5155

ALAN BUSHSBAUM
40 Hudson Street
New York, NY 10013
212•608•0185

DIMITRI BULAZEL
AIA Architects
26 Ferncliff Road
Cos Cob, CT 06807
203•869•3782

HARIET ECKSTEIN
One Fifth Avenue
New York, NY 10003
212•475•0045

DAN FRIEDMAN
℅ Art et Industrie
594 Broadway
New York, NY 10012
212•431•1661
and
Neotu
123 Greene Street
New York, NY 10012
212•982•0205

MICHAEL HASKINS ASSOCIATES
435 Park Avenue
New York, NY 10016
212•696•0552

STEVEN HOLL
435 Hudson Street
New York, NY 10014
212•989•0918

JACK LENOR LARSEN
41 East 11 Street
New York, NY 10003•4685
212•674•3993

HEATON LONNECKER ASSOC. ARCHITECTS
3270 Sul Ross
Houston, TX 77908
713•526•0200

MACHADO AND SILVETTI
560 Harrison Avenue
Boston, MA 02118
617▪426▪7070

THOMAS MAYNE
MICHAEL ROTONDI
1718 2nd Street
Santa Monica, CA 90404
213▪477▪2674

CHARLES MOORE
Moore, Ruble, Yudell
930 Pico Blvd.
Santa Monica, CA 90405
213▪450▪1400

MORSA
247 Centre Street
New York, NY 10013
212▪226▪4324

MURPHY/JAHN
35 East Wacker Drive
Chicago, IL 60601
312▪427▪7300

PRESTON PHILIPS
P.O. Box AM
Bridgehampton, NY 11932
516▪537▪1237

DAN PHIPPS AND ASSOCIATES
131 Post Street
San Francisco, CA 94109
415▪776▪1606

PETER SHIRE
1930 Echo Park Avenue
Los Angeles, CA 90026
213▪662▪5385

SITE PROJECTS, INC.
65 Bleecker Street
New York, NY 10012
212▪254▪8300

LEE SOLNICK
132 West 21 Street
New York, NY 10011
212▪989▪2624

HENRY SMITH▪MILLER
305 Canal Street
New York, NY 10013
212▪996▪3875

ROBERT VENTURI
Venturi, Rauch & Scott Brown
4236 Main Street
Philadelphia, PA 19127
215▪487▪0400

JOY WULKE
85 Willow Street
New Haven, CT 06511
203▪481▪6693

PAINTERS AND SURFACE FINISH STUDIOS

LESLEY ACHITOFF
160 West End Avenue
New York, NY 10023
212▪496▪0462

VIRGINIA CRAWFORD
285 West Broadway
New York, NY 10013
212▪226▪6259

EVERGREENE PAINTING STUDIOS, INC.
635 West 23 Street
New York, NY 10011
212▪727▪9500

RICHARD GILLETTE &
STEPHEN SHADLEY
144 West 27 Street
New York, NY 10001
212▪243▪6913

RICHARD HAAS
361 West 36 Street
New York, NY 10018
212▪947▪9868

ANNIE KELLY
6938 Camrose Drive
Los Angeles, Ca 90068
213▪876▪5374

LILLIAN KENNEDY
319 Park Place
Brooklyn, NY 11238
718▪622▪2840

NANCY A. KINTISCH
89 Bridge Street
Brooklyn, NY 11201
718▪935▪9019

PAMELA MARGONELLI
303 Greenwich Street
New York, NY 10013
212▪233▪0559

THOMAS MASARYK
515 40 Street
2nd floor
Brooklyn, NY 11232
718▪853▪4940

SERPENTINE STUDIO LTD.
453 Greenwich Street
New York, NY 10013
212▪925▪7610

MICHAEL THORNTON-SMITH
123 Chambers St.
New York, NY 10007
212▪619▪5338

TROMPLOY, INC.
119 West 25th Street
New York, NY 10011
212▪366▪5579

STENCILERS

EVERGREENE PAINTING STUDIOS, INC.
635 West 23 Street
New York, NY 10011
212▪727▪9500

LYNN GOODPASTURE
42 West 17 Street
New York, NY 10010
212▪645▪5334

CILE LORD
42 East 12 Street
New York, NY 10003
212▪757▪2774

LESLIE ANN POWERS
241 State Street
Guildford, CT 06437
203▪453▪9583

LAURA TORBET STUDIO
225 East 73 Street
New York, NY 10021
212▪988▪2898

TROMPLOY, INC.
119 West 25 Street
New York, NY 10003
212▪366▪5579

TILES

DISH IS IT
Box 162
3301½ Mission Street
San Francisco, CA 94110
415▪558▪8453

DOROTHY HAFNER
44 Cooper Square
New York, NY 10003
212•677•9797

ITALIAN TILE CENTER
499 Park Avenue
New York, NY 10022
212•226•4375

JOYCE KOZLOFF
152 Wooster Street
New York, NY 10012
212•673•7235

NINA YANKOWITZ
106 Spring Street
2nd floor
New York, NY 10012
212•226•4375

GLASS ARTISTS

MARNI BAKST
235 East Fifth Street
New York, NY 10003
212•533•2556

PATSY NORVELL
78 Greene Street
New York, NY 10012
212•431•5341

WALLPAPERS AND FABRICS

ART PEOPLE
594 Broadway
New York, NY 10012
212•431•4828

BRADBURY & BRADBURY
P.O. Box 155
Benica, CA 94510
707•746•1900

CHINA SEAS
152 Madison Avenue
Suite 1400
New York, NY 10016
212•420•1170

GROUNDWORKS
A Division of Lee Jofa
979 Third Avenue
New York, NY 10021
212•759•8250

SCALAMANDRE
37•24 24 Street
Long Island City, NY 11101
718•361•8500

TAPESTRIES AND WALLHANGINGS

KRIS DEY
The Allrich Gallery
251 Post Street
San Francisco, CA 94108
415•398•8896

MODERN MASTER TAPESTRIES
11 East 57 Street
New York, NY 10022
212•838•0412

ANNE McKENZIE NICKOLSON
5020 North Illinois
Indianapolis, IN 46208
317•257•8929

RUTH SCHEUER
Scheuer Tapestry Studio
167 Spring Street
New York, NY 10012
212•431•7500

CYNTHIA SCHIRA
Miller/Brown Gallery
355 Hayes Street
San Francisco, CA 94102
415•861•2028

SCREENS

GRETCHEN BELLINGER INC.
P.O. Box 64/31 Ontario Street
Cohoes, NY 12047
518•235•2828

KATHERINE CHENEY HUMPSTONE
165 Hudson Street
New York, NY 10013
212•966•1556

CATHERINE CREAMER
C/W Studios
41 Union Square West
New York, NY 10003
212•255•6210

JACK LENOR LARSEN
41 East 11 Street
New York, NY 10003
212•674•3993

PATSY NORVELL
78 Greene Street
New York, NY 10012
212•431•5341

JACK RADETSKY
℅ OK Harris Gallery
383 West Broadway
New York, NY 10012
212•431•3600

ARLENE SLAVIN
119 East 18 Street
New York, NY 10003
212•777•3042

CANADIAN

PAINTERS AND SURFACE FINISH STUDIOS

ANSELMO ART STUDIO
280 Avenue Road
Toronto, ON M4V 2G7
416•966•3856

LA BOITE DU PINCEAU D'ARLEQUIN
760, rue St. Felix
Montréal, PQ H3L 2B8
514•878•9166

COLLECTORS CUSTOM FURNITURE
8920 Shaunessey Street
Vancouver, BC V6P 3Y5
604•321•5171

FAMOUS PAINTERS
5785 Victoria Drive
Vancouver, BC V5P 3W5
604•324•1923

FINE ARTISTS AT WORK
#1A–1215 13th Street SE
Calgary, AB T2G 3J4
403•263•2877

FREESTYLE DECORATIVE FINISHES
℅ 4945 Lochside Drive
Victoria, BC V8Y 2E6
604•385•8131

RICHARD GORDON
174 Neville Park Blvd.
Toronto, ON M4E 3P8
416•690•2644

JANNA DECORATORS
580 Front Street West
Toronto, ON M5V 1C1
416•467•0624

LAPRES & LAPRES
#3–2256 West 3rd Avenue
Vancouver, BC V6K 1M1
604•736•1150

MASTER HAND PAINTING & DECORATING
321 John Street
Nanaimo, BC V9S 5K1
604•753•0016

MARIO NOVIELLO
#3–7 Fraser Avenue
Toronto, OH M6K 1Y9
416•531•5328

WESTERN WALLPRINTING
#4–7419 50th Avenue
Calgary, AB T4P 1M5
403•236•4559

WOOD ART PRODUCTS
70 Snidecrost Road, Unit M
Toronto, ON L4K 2K3
416•660•3839

WALLPAPERS AND FABRICS

A1 LINEN CHEST
2305 Rockland Centre
Montréal, PQ H3P 3E9
514•341•7810

AVANT-GARDE FABRICS LTD
7955, Rue Alfred
Anjou, PQ H1J 1J3
1•800•361•8886

CHARLES RUPERT DESIGNS
2004 Oak Bay Avenue
Victoria, BC V8R 1E4
604•592•4916

CHINTZ AND CO.
1180 Marine Drive
North Vancouver, BC V7P 1S8
604•381•2404

CHINTZ AND CO.
1120–10th Avenue SW
Calgary, AB T2R 0B6
403•245•3449

CHINTZY'S
10340–134th Street
Edmonton, AB T5N 2B1
403•453•2212

EGAN-LAING
315–1080 Mainland Street
Vancouver, BC V6B 2T4
604•688•2249

EGAN-LAING
1067 Westport Crescent
Mississauga, ON L5T 1E8
416•678•9131

FORBO-SELECT WALL COVERING LTD.
106 East 7th Avenue
Vancouver, BC V5T 1N6
604•872•8181

LIONS WALLCOVERINGS & FABRICS INC.
265 Davenport Road
Toronto, ON M5R 1K5
416•924•7779

MILL WALLCOVERINGS
8380 River Road
Ladner, BC V4G 1B5
604•946•2130

REMBOURRAGE CREATIF
1751 Richardson Street, #7325
Montreal, PQ H3K 1G6
514•939•2455

VISION TEXTILES INC.
100 Port Royal East
Montréal, PQ H3L 1H7
514▪381▪5941

WALLS ALIVE
10803–124th Street
Edmonton, AB T5M 0H4
403▪452▪8201

YESTERYEAR FURNISHINGS
15 St. Peters Street
Parkdale, PEI C1A 4N1
902▪368▪3722

SUPPLIES

CLASSIC ARCHITECTURAL COATINGS
2700 Dufferin Street
Toronto, ON M6B 3R1
416▪789▪7887

MULTIFLEK PAINT SYSTEMS INC.
111 Granton Drive
Richmond Hill, ON L4B 1L5
416▪886▪9733

TILES AND MARBLE

CERAMIC DECOR ONTARIO LTD.
4544 Dufferin Street
Downsview, ON M3H 5R9
416▪665▪8787

COUNTRY TILES
321 Davenport Road
Toronto, ON M5R 1K5
416▪922▪9214

OLYMPIA FLOOR & WALL TILE CO.
1000 Lawrence Avenue West
Toronto, ON M6B 4A8
416▪789▪4122

ROCKFORD MARBLE CENTRE LTD.
160 Pears Avenue
Toronto, ON M5R 1T2
416▪922▪6122

ANN SACKS TILE & STONE
2349 Granville Street
Vancouver, BC V6H 3G4
604▪737▪7966

STEPTOE & WIFE ANTIQUES
322 Geary Avenue
Toronto, ON M6H 2C7
416▪530▪4200

TMT MARBLE SUPPLY
900 Keele Street
Toronto, ON M6N 3E7
416▪653▪6111

PHOTO CREDITS

© Peter Aaron/Esto: 20, 21, 62, 94, 106, 112–113, 122, 126–127
Lesley Achitoff: 17 left
Jade Albert: 31
Art People: 72
A2Z: 111
Marni Bakst: 69, 70 left, 70–71
Gretchen Bellinger Inc: 98, 99
Michelle Bello, Courtesy of the Allrich Gallery: 90–91
Roger Bester, Courtesy of Groundworks: 79 upper left
Peter Blaikie: 89
Bradbury & Bradbury: 76, 77, 82, 83, 132
Jere Cockrell: 74, 75
© Dan Cornish/Esto: 124 upper left
Nick Edwards: 34, 105
George Erml: 56
Evergreene Studios: 18–19
Eliot Fine: 58–59
Ron Forth: 54
Brett Froomer: 30
GF 55 Architects: 57
Lynn Goodpasture, design © Lynn Goodpasture 1980: 45
Robert Grant: 98
Rob Gray: 17 right
Paul Hesler: 102–103
© Wolfgang Hoyt/Esto: 33
Hudson River Museum: 104, 105
Christopher Irion: 52
Alan P. Jacobs, design © Lynn Goodpasture: 64 upper left, 64–65
Ned Johnston: 101
Howard Kaplan: 44
Lillian Kennedy: 32
Christopher Little: 50, 51
Peter Margonelli: 23 upper right, 24–25
© Peter Mauss/Esto: 28–29, 37
Norman McGrath: 61 upper right, 67 upper right, 116, 117
Miller Brown Gallery: 88
Modern Master Tapestries: 84, 86, 87
Steve Moore: 108, 108–109
Hans Namuth: 47
Anne McKenzie Nickolson: 92, 93
O.K. Harris Gallery: 100
Robert Perron: 46, 61 lower left
N. Rodriguez: 16 upper left
Marc Roscams: 26
Barry Rosenthal: 22, 23 lower left
Lee Skolnick: 112 upper left
Werner Stegemayer: 78, 79 lower right
James Steinkamp: 120, 121
© Ezra Stoller/Esto: 114
Tim Street-Porter: 16 lower right, 18, 55, 66–67, 97, 118, 119, 125, 128, 129, 138
Studio Leiman, Courtesy of Alan Buchsbaum: 11, 14–15
Michael Thornton-Smith: 35
Laura Torbet: 40, 42–43
Anne Turyn: 60
Courtesy of Tromploy: 10
Victoria and Albert Museum: 80–81
Bob Wagner: 96
© Paul Warchol/Esto: 12, 48 left, 48–49, 68, 126 left
Bruce Wolf: 36, 38, 39

References to captions are printed in italic type.

INDEX